Shaba II:
The French and Belgian Intervention in Zaire in 1978

by
Lieutenant Colonel Thomas P. Odom

U.S. Army Command and General Staff College
Fort Leavenworth, Kansas 66027-6900

COMBAT STUDIES INSTITUTE

Library of Congress Cataloging-in-Publication Data

Odom, Thomas P. (Thomas Paul), 1953-
    Shaba II : the French and Belgian intervention in Zaire in 1978 /
by Thomas P. Odom.
        p.   cm.
    Includes bibliographical references.
    1. Zaire—History–Shaba Uprising, 1978.   2. Kolwezi Massacre,
Kolwezi, Zaire, 1978.   3. Zaire—Foreign relations—France.
4. France—Foreign relations—Zaire.   5. Zaire—Foreign
relations—Belgium.   6. Belgium—Foreign relations—Zaire.   I. Title.
II. Title: Shaba two.
DT658.25.036 1992
967.5103—dc20   92-29132
                                                                        CIP

CONTENTS

Illustrations v

    I. Introduction 1

   II. Origins 3

  III. Shaba I 17

  IV. Shaba II Begins 31

   V. Massacre in Kolwezi 43

  VI. The West Reacts 57

 VII. The Evacuation of Kisangani: "Stanleyville II" 73

VIII. Conclusions 91

Appendix

   A. Personalities, Terms, and Acronyms 99

   B. Chronology 105

   C. Organizational Charts of French and Belgian Units
       in Zaire 111

Notes 113

Bibliography 129

ILLUSTRATIONS

Maps

1. Zaire and the bordering countries 4
2. The FNLC's first invasion into Shaba, March 1977 18
3. The FNLC's second invasion into Shaba, May 1978 32
4. Kolwezi, 17 May 1978 51
5. Kolwezi, 19 May 1978 62
6. Kolwezi, 20 May 1978 78
7. Metal-Shaba 83

I. INTRODUCTION

Another dawn broke in the Zairian mining town of Kolwezi on 13 May 1978. Normally on the Saturday before Pentecost, the 3,000 foreign residents would be anticipating a relaxing weekend at home or with friends and family at the nearby lake. Most would have slept late and enjoyed the day off. In any case, no one would have expected to do anything in a hurry. After all, one who works in Africa soon comes to embrace its pace of life.

But the 13th was not to be just another day for Kolwezi. The town had been through a restless evening; an atmosphere of tension had hung over the city. Dogs had barked all night, and the expatriates found themselves waking repeatedly to glance at bedside clocks in anticipation of morning.

By 0500, the sun was climbing. Some of the foreigners were awake and preparing breakfast. Some looking out their doors found the streets unusually empty for a market day, when everyone tries to be the first customer and get the best price. The streets were not empty for long, however. Shortly after dawn, firing broke out in different parts of the city. That, in itself, was not too disturbing. The Zairian Army was known for its habit of firing ammunition for all sorts of reasons. But when the firing grew in intensity and Zairian soldiers began running through the streets pursued by soldiers in different uniforms, it was clear that this would not be just another weekend in Kolwezi.

Death had descended on the mining town, and many of its residents, native and foreign, had less than a week left to live. Soon, the city would become a charnel house with several hundred dead scattered through its streets. Four different armies would clash in Kolwezi during the coming days. Once again, people would shake their heads and mutter, "C'est l'Afrique!"

Since the end of World War II, the use of the threat of terrorism—particularly that of hostage taking—has grown increasingly serious. Governments have struggled to find the best means of dealing with such episodes, and the burden has often fallen on military forces. When one mentions hostage rescues, people are usually reminded of the daring Entebbe rescue by the Israelis or the less fortunate Desert One attempt by the United States. Few know of the Dragon operations in 1964 by the Belgian Paracommando Regiment and the U.S. Air Force, the first hostage rescues since World War II. The Dragon missions were the longest in range and the most successful operations,

1

saving over 2,000 hostages from execution by the Simba rebels in the Democratic Republic of the Congo.

Of those few who recall the Dragon operations of 1964, even fewer realize that 1978 saw a repeat performance by the Belgian Paracommando Regiment along with France's 2éme Régiment Étranger de Parachutistes (2d R.E.P.). In May 1978, the French, the Belgians, and the Zairian armed forces were forced to rescue expatriates in the mining center of Kolwezi, Zaire. The operations that ensued could by no means be called combined operations, as political differences prohibited cooperation among the forces involved. Instead, each country conducted independent operations, providing a truly unique opportunity for military analysts and historians to study each military's approach to the crisis in Zaire.

II. ORIGINS

Even to the casual observer, Africa in 1978 was ablaze with war. The continent was the scene of conflict from one end to the other. Wars raged in Namibia, Angola, Chad, Rhodesia, and the Spanish Sahara. The Ogaden, on the Horn of Africa, and Mozambique struggled to recover from the destruction of war. Meanwhile, Tanzania and Uganda prepared to engage in open conflict. Yet this level of war was hardly unprecedented: Africa had always been a violent and mysterious place. Zaire, the setting for Joseph Conrad's *Heart of Darkness*, was no stranger to the ravages of war or to violence.[1]

Zaire, the former Belgian Congo, joined the ranks of independent countries as the Democratic Republic of the Congo on 30 June 1960 (see map 1). A Belgian colony for almost ninety years, the Congo was ill-prepared by its colonial masters for the independence its leaders had demanded. Within days of independence, the country plunged into a maelstrom of war that continued, almost without pause, for the next five years. From 1960 to 1963, the United Nations struggled to maintain the territorial integrity of the Congo against Belgian-sponsored attempts to wrest the mineral-rich province of Katanga (Shaba) from the control of Leopoldville (Kinshasa). With the help of a mercenary-reinforced Katangan Gendarmerie led by Belgian officers under Colonel Frédéric J. L. A. Vandewalle, Moise Tshombe, the provincial leader, fought the Congo's central government and the United Nations to a standstill. Only with U.S. pressure on Belgium to reduce its support to Tshombe did the United Nations finally succeed in forcing the collapse of Tshombe's Katangan state.[2]

With Tshombe's defeat in 1963, the Katangan Gendarmerie crossed the border into Portuguese Angola and what seemed permanent exile. Maintaining its military organization and some of its mercenary leaders, it nevertheless waited for an opportunity to return home. Like the majority of the population of Katanga province, the Katangan Gendarmerie was primarily Lunda in tribal origin and easily fit into the areas of Angola that were also Lunda. The opportunity to return to the Congo, however, came quickly. In early 1964, a new wave of rebellion swept across the Congo and, this time, Moise Tshombe, the former provincial dissident, was called on to rescue the struggling central government.[3]

Continued tribal dissatisfaction with the government in Leopoldville had led to an outbreak of rebellion in the closing months of 1963. Heavy-handed repression by the Armée Nationale Congolaise (ANC), the fledgling national army, coupled with the United Nations'

3

Map 1. Zaire and the bordering countries

withdrawal of its peacekeeping forces in early 1964, had produced a new outbreak of terror in the Congo. Unable to contain the spreading troubles, the Congolese president, Joseph Kasavubu, asked Tshombe to return from his European exile to assume the office of prime minister. Agreeing, Tshombe came back in mid-1964 to a rapidly deteriorating situation. In August 1964, the rebels, or Simbas, had taken most of the eastern Congo, including the regional capital of Stanleyville (Kisangani).

The seizure of Stanleyville doomed the rebellion because it prodded the United States and Belgium into supporting Tshombe's efforts against the Simbas. Once the rebels seized Stanleyville and its 1,600 foreigners, Western intervention was inevitable. Building slowly, that response began with the recall of the Katangan Gendarmerie and the recruitment of mercenaries to lead them. Much like the original formation of the Katangan Gendarmerie in the fight for secession, the operation owed much to the organizational skills of Colonel Vandewalle, who along with a levy of Belgian advisers was once again in the Congo at the side of Moise Tshombe. After a period of organization and training, Vandewalle unleashed his forces against the Simbas and, with the support of Central Intelligence Agency (CIA) aircraft and Cuban-exile pilots, he soon was ready to take Stanleyville.[4]

Vandewalle's success in retaking rebel-held territory forced the United States and Belgium to intervene militarily against the Simbas. Most of the 1,600 expatriates in Stanleyville were Belgian, but 5 were American diplomats, whom the rebels began to threaten as Vandewalle's campaign gained ground. As his drive on Stanleyville gained momentum, the rebels seized the Belgians as hostages. Unable to halt Vandewalle short of withdrawing all support from Tshombe, the United States and Belgium agonizingly decided to use direct military force to rescue the non-Congolese in Stanleyville and perhaps other areas as well.

Staging from Europe, the Belgian Paracommando Regiment and the U.S. Air Force conducted Operation Dragon Rouge to rescue the hostages. Using 5 U.S. Air Force C-130s to drop 340 paras on the airport, the operation succeeded in rescuing most of the non-Congolese on 24 November 1964. Following Vandewalle's arrival in the city that same day, the Paracommandos hastily planned and executed a second operation, Dragon Noir, at Paulis (Isiro) on 26 November. Fearing an international uproar and deepening involvement in the situation, the combined force withdrew within days, leaving hundreds of other non-Congolese behind rebel lines. Many of these unfortunates suffered hideous deaths at the hands of the Simbas, which was long remembered in Brussels.[5]

Although the Dragon operations broke the Simba movement, the war continued little abated into the next year. The Katangans remained in the thick of it alongside the mercenaries. Frustrated with the struggle, Leopoldville declared the rebellion over in March 1965. Notwithstanding this declaration, the rebels continued fighting in scattered areas over the next decade. Nevertheless, Tshombe and his

Katangan army had succeeded, with heavy foreign assistance, in saving the Democratic Republic of the Congo.

Success, however, does not always bring reward in Congolese politics. With the war over, squabbling between Tshombe and his former sponsor increased. Kasavubu, jealous of Tshombe's success and suspicious of his intentions, dismissed him from the government in October 1965, but that action only intensified the struggle as Congolese leaders split into pro- and anti-Tshombe camps. Disgusted with the infighting and more than a little opportunistic, the commander in chief of the ANC, Lieutenant General Joseph Mobutu, seized power and declared himself president.[6]

Mobutu had been a fixture in Congolese politics since the early days of independence. Befriended by the country's stormy and short-lived first prime minister, Patrice Lumumba, Mobutu became the first chief of staff of the ANC. From that point on, Mobutu served as a power broker behind the throne. Based on his control of the military (which, despite its bad performance in the field, was still important in Leopoldville), Mobutu held enormous influence in the government, and he had proved his willingness to wield that power in September 1960 by temporarily seizing power to halt a struggle between Kasavubu and Lumumba.[7]

During the next five years, Mobutu struggled to build the ANC into something of a fighting force. Born out of the ashes of the Force Publique, the ANC was a uniformed military disaster. Soon after the revolt of the Force Publique against the Belgians, Prime Minister Lumumba had promoted all the men and officers of the newly formed army several ranks in order to ensure their support. Renaming the Force Publique army the Armée Nationale Congolaise, Lumumba soon had to rely on it to put down the Katangan secession. Here, the ANC proved incapable. Tshombe's Katangan Gendarmerie humiliated the ANC and aroused Mobutu's ire. That resentment grew when Tshombe brought his Katangans back in 1964 to save the ANC and the Congo.[8]

Mobutu's 1965 coup was daring, for it challenged Tshombe when he was strongest. Tshombe had almost 18,000 gendarmes and several hundred mercenaries available to support him against Mobutu and the ANC. But Mobutu's forces were concentrated in the Leopoldville area, and he was able to consolidate his power quickly. Tshombe publicly supported the new president and then wisely departed for Europe, where he soon began scheming to resume power.[9]

For the Katangan Gendarmerie, Mobutu's coup and Tshombe's extended vacation in Europe did not bode well. Though the war

Mobutu Sese Seko

against the Simbas was officially over, the ANC and the gendarmes were still fighting against the rebels who failed to heed Leopoldville's decrees. The alliance between the ANC and the Katangans remained uneasy however, and tension gradually increased, exacerbated by tribal hatreds and linguistic differences.

The situation exploded in Stanleyville in 1966 with the revolt of the Katangan Gendarmerie's Baka Regiment. Led by Colonel Ferdinand Tshipola, the regiment was one of the original units that had returned from Angola in 1964. Seizing the airport, the mutineers resisted government offers to negotiate a settlement for two months. Finally, Robert Denard and an all-white mercenary unit put down the rebellion—for a substantial cash bonus. Meanwhile, Mobutu accused Tshombe of using the revolt to generate support for his return to power. Yet others believed that Tshombe was not connected to this attempt. Rather, the 1966 mutiny was a Katangan reaction to rumors that the unit might be disbanded.[10]

In contrast, the mercenary revolt of 1967 was directly tied to a plot to return Tshombe to power. Unfortunately for the mutineers and even more so for Tshombe, the wily Katangan's luck had finally deserted him. By the time of the revolt on 5 July 1967, Tshombe was languishing in an Algerian prison, the victim of a hijacking operation apparently sponsored by Mobutu. Two years later, the Algerians announced Tshombe's death of a heart attack, a report questioned by many. Nevertheless, after the mercenaries learned that they were to be disbanded by the ANC, Jean Schramme, the infamous Belgian planter turned mercenary, came forward to lead the revolt.[11]

On 5 July, Schramme, 11 whites, and some 100 Katangans began the mutiny in Stanleyville by firing on an ANC camp full of troops and their families. The slaughter was terrible, and the ANC reacted by killing thirty other mercenaries who were not involved. The rest of the mercenaries immediately joined Schramme. After weeks of fighting, Schramme withdrew from Stanleyville with a force of around 150 mercenaries and 1,000 black troops, not all of whom had been trained. The rebel force conducted a fighting retreat to Bukavu. Arriving there on 8 August, Schramme's force had bloodied the ANC repeatedly and continued to grow.

Schramme held onto Bukavu for seven weeks. Repeatedly defeating ANC units thrown against him, Schramme humiliated Mobutu and destroyed the little cohesiveness that remained in the ANC. Tribal conflicts began to appear as ANC soldiers from Katanga took the blame for the defeats. T-28s flying missions against the mutineers mistakenly attacked ANC forces. In addition, attacks failed due to a lack of artillery ammunition, and at least one ANC battalion revolted in sheer frustration over continuous fiascoes.

Finally, the ANC began to make progress. Fresh units, including a paratroop unit, arrived by American airlift. Rearmed, resupplied, and reinforced, 15,000 ANC troops began to push inside Bukavu. Schramme's men had been cut off for almost two months, and casualties were growing. Denard attempted to reach Schramme by crossing the Angolan border with a mixed force of eighty mercenaries and gendarmes on bicycles, but ANC air attacks drove them back. On 29 October, the ANC launched its final assault on the city. After seven days, the survivors in Schramme's force crossed the border into Rwanda.[12]

Not surprisingly, the ANC considered the operation a great victory. Mobutu had long hoped for an improvement in his army's martial standing. Suddenly, the ANC could claim that it had defeated an internal enemy without foreign assistance. The American airlift aside, the claim was true and, in light of the ANC's previous record, rather remarkable. The fact that a force of several hundred mercenaries and 1,000 Katangans conducted a fighting withdrawal over several hundred miles and then repelled attacks by 15,000 troops for nearly 2 months was conveniently forgotten.[13]

In contrast, the Katangan Gendarmerie did not forget its successes against the ANC or Mobutu's vengeance. The Katangan survivors of the Bukavu battle later were offered amnesty and repatriation to the Congo only to disappear mysteriously shortly after their return. Most observers agree that they were executed. Meanwhile, Mobutu's governor in Katanga carried out reprisals against the entire province and purged the provincial police of all the former Katangan Gendarmerie. Joined by refugees, the ex-gendarmes crossed the border into Angola. A decade later, they would have the opportunity for revenge.[14]

Following his victory at Bukavu, Mobutu concentrated on consolidating his position within the country. In keeping with its policy of maintaining access to the country's vast mineral resources, the West had consistently worked to keep the country from collapsing. The biggest backers had been and still were Belgium and the United States. Following Belgium's withdrawal of support from Tshombe's Katangan secession, the two Western allies had cooperated closely in their support of the Congo.

After the collapse of the Simba Rebellion and subsequent mercenary revolts, Belgium nearly lost its predominance in the Congo's mining industry. The Union Minière du Haut-Katanga (UMHK), the Belgian mining company founded in 1906, found itself at cross-purposes with Mobutu in 1966 over the control it could exert over the country without government sanction. The problem surfaced when UMHK raised prices on its products without consulting Leopoldville. Mobutu, who had already indicated that the country was going to move toward more government controls over private industry, responded with a law requiring all companies established before independence to reapply for their charters. When UMHK did so, Mobutu denied the application and ordered that the company's assets be seized to form the government-owned corporation, Générale Congolaise des Minerais (GECOMIN). Since GECOMIN could not operate without Belgian and European technicians, the Congolese signed an agreement that offered the Belgians 6 percent of the gross revenues in return for operating the mines. Renamed Générale des Carrières et des Mines (GECAMINES) in 1971, the company ensured that a substantial expatriate population would remain concentrated in the Congo's mining region despite government efforts to replace them with trained locals.[15]

Belgium's relations with Mobutu remained stormy. Many problems were to be expected between a former colony and its European master, but Mobutu's attempts to break with the colonial past were at times excessive. Mobutu aspired to be known as an African nationalist, and his program of "authenticity" was the first step toward that goal. He began renaming everything in the country that had a European name or a strong association with the Congo's colonial past. The Democratic Republic of the Congo became Zaire, and the Congo River became the Zaire River. Town names changed: Leopoldville became Kinshasa; Stanleyville, Kisangani; and Elizabethville, Lubumbashi. Mobutu even changed his own name. But when he threatened to give five years in jail to a Catholic priest who baptized a Zairian with a European name, conflict erupted. As if this were not enough to challenge the Church and strongly Catholic Belgium, Mobutu declared that Christmas would henceforth be celebrated in June. He stepped up the challenge by nationalizing the schools, but when the school system collapsed without the support of the missionaries, he asked them to return. In 1974, when Julius Chromé, a Belgian lawyer, published a book in Brussels criticizing Mobutu, the Zairian president demanded that the Belgian government confiscate the book. When Brussels refused, "spontaneous" demonstrations occurred outside the Belgian Embassy. Belgium then recalled its ambassador. Relations between the two countries deteriorated further as Zairian dissidents increasingly used Brussels as a base of operations.[16]

In 1974, Mobutu's programs developed real problems. He moved his authenticity program into the small business sector by nationalizing all foreign-owned enterprises. After seizing hundreds of farms, trading posts, and other businesses, Mobutu turned them over, as political payoffs, to untrained Zairians, who failed miserably in running them. In this heavy-handed move, Mobutu had inadvertently caused Zaire's rural production and distribution system to collapse. His timing could not have been worse: in 1974, the price of copper, Zaire's main export, declined 50 percent, and the country went from prosperity to bankruptcy almost overnight. Zaire's Western backers were left holding loans that would require drastic rescheduling to keep the country from collapsing. When the International Monetary Fund agreed to manage Zaire's central bank as part of the rescheduling process, its auditors found that corruption had contributed to Zaire's economic crisis: 40 percent of the government's funds were filling private accounts. Mobutu's vision of Zairianization was turning into disaster.[17]

Mobutu faced other problems beyond Zaire's economic collapse. Undeterred by the Katangan Gendarmerie still waiting across the border in Angola, Mobutu continued to make new enemies. Some opposition groups were veteran opponents; the African Socialist Forces (FSA) and the People's Revolutionary Party (PRP) had formed in 1964 after the fall of Stanleyville. The National Movement for the Liberation of the Congo, also Marxist-Leninist, dated back to 1965. In extending his Zairianization program to the political field, Mobutu had swept aside all political parties to establish a single party, the Popular Movement of the Revolution (MPR). In 1974, Mobutu rammed through a new constitution that formally centralized virtually all power in his hands. His assumption of the title "Le Guide" further triggered the appearance of new opposition groups. The Democratic Forces for the Liberation of the Congo (FODELICO) coalesced around Antoine Gizenga and other survivors of the 1964 rebellion. Members of the MPR broke away to form the Action Movement for the Resurrection of the Congo (MARC). Mobutu seemed to be in trouble.[18]

However, those who predicted that Mobutu would slow down on his Zairianization programs in the face of growing Western, Church, and internal opposition were wrong. At the end of 1974, Mobutu visited the People's Republic of China and returned sporting a new Mao jacket and the title of "Citizen Mobutu." Proclaiming his intent to "radicalize the Zairian revolution," he expanded the nationalization programs to include many of the Zairianized businesses he had just given away. Other well-considered measures included a 50 percent cut in all rents and caps on salaries. It was too much, and in June, members of the military, now called the Forces Armées Zairoise (FAZ), attempted a coup. The bid failed, and after a brief trial, some eleven officers and thirty civilians were convicted and jailed. Mobutu publicly accused the United States of sponsoring the attempt.[19]

Mobutu's challenge to the United States represented the low point of his relationship with Washington. Like Belgium, the United States had been growing steadily more concerned with Mobutu's Zairianization. His nationalization policies and his break in relations with Israel in 1973 added to the tension. Following Mobutu's criticism in January 1975 of the U.S. failure to act against apartheid—despite his own contacts with the Republic of South Africa—estrangement between the two countries seemed a distinct possibility. With Mobutu's accusations in June, the United States withdrew its ambassador.[20]

It seemed in mid-1975 that Mobutu's future as Zaire's leader was propelling him along a path leading away from his traditional Western

Jonas Savimbi, charismatic leader of UNITA

base of support. Zaire seemed doomed to economic ruin, and "Citizen Mobutu" appeared determined to alienate all who might be willing to rescue the country from itself. Mobutu, however, was already involved in events in Angola that would assure him of continued Western support at the cost of three wars.

The Portuguese African Empire was nearing its end in 1974. For years, the Portuguese had been fighting Angolan nationalists seeking to gain control of their own country. By 1974, three different groups had emerged in the struggle: the National Front for the Liberation of Angola (FNLA) led by Holden Roberto, the National Union for the Total Independence of Angola (UNITA) headed by Jonas Savimbi, and the Popular Movement for the Liberation of Angola (MPLA) under Agostino Neto.[21]

A coup by the Portuguese Army in April indicated that an end to the anticolonial struggle was near, but it left still at issue who would control Angola. The FNLA, UNITA, and MPLA were deeply suspicious of each other. Roberto's FNLA espoused a nationalist line and drew its greatest support from the north of the country among the Kongo tribe. UNITA likewise was a nationalist organization and was tribally affiliated, in this case with the Ovimbundu in the south. The MPLA tended heavily toward Marxist-Leninist dogma and depended heavily on Soviet and Cuban support. Most of the MPLA followers were of the intelligentsia, mulattoes, and others around Luanda. None of these groups were inclined to cooperate with the others.[22]

Mobutu had long supported the Angolan guerrillas. He favored Roberto and had provided arms and training for the FNLA. In fact, Roberto was his relative by marriage. Mobutu wanted to ensure that a friendly Angola emerged on Zaire's southern border, and he went so far as to attempt to negotiate a coalition government of transition incorporating the FNLA, UNITA, and a breakaway faction of the MPLA. When the Portuguese backers for the plan fell victim to a second coup, Mobutu tried a more direct approach.[23]

Mobutu, who had a number of advantages, decided on direct military intervention against the MPLA. In sheer numbers, the FNLA was the strongest of the groups, with over 10,000 men in training

Angolan President Agostino Neto

Cuban instructors (foreground) with MPLA recruits at training camp near Luanda

camps and 2,000 inside Angola. Mobutu had convinced both the United States and the People's Republic of China to support the FNLA, and both countries were busy supplying weapons and money. He also looked to a UNITA-FNLA accommodation based on their common hatred of the MPLA. Furthermore, the South Africans could be counted on to support UNITA from the south, as they, too, were afraid of a Communist regime in Angola. Finally, Mobutu assumed that the FAZ, with its steady buildup in men and modern weapons, would do well.[24]

Between July and August 1975, a total of five FAZ battalions crossed the borders into Angola and Cabinda. By October, FNLA and FAZ units were only twenty miles from Luanda. Meanwhile, a South African, FNLA, and UNITA column pushed up from the south. Everything was going well until November, when suddenly the resistance outside Luanda hardened. Mobutu's old foe, the Katangan Gendarmerie, had taken a hand in the war.[25]

Following the defeat of the 1967 mercenary revolt and Mobutu's reprisals against the people of Katanga, most of the Katangan Gendarmerie had once again gone south into exile. The Portuguese had used them to fight the spreading rebellion, creating counterinsurgency units under the command of ex-Katangan police general, Nathaniel Mbumba. Called the Black Arrows, the ex-gendarmes were useful in offsetting Mobutu's support of the FNLA, and in June 1968, they assumed the title of the Front for the National Liberation of the Congo (FNLC). When the end of Portuguese rule appeared near, the FNLC allied itself with the MPLA rather than trust a Mobutu offer of amnesty. An alliance of survival for the FNLC, it proved critical in saving the MPLA.[26]

Now just when Mobutu seemed about to take the winner's pot in his Angolan gamble, the FNLC seized the opportunity for revenge. Reequipped and trained by the Cubans, the ex-gendarmes slowed the FAZ-FNLA offensive and allowed the Cubans to bring in troops, armor, and aircraft. The near FAZ-FNLA victory turned into disaster. The invaders fell apart and raced back across the border, pausing only long enough to loot abandoned houses along the way. On 28 February 1976, Mobutu and Neto signed the Brazzaville Accords to end the conflict and to end support for dissident groups operating inside each other's borders. It was a futile instrument.[27]

The Angolan adventure was a total disaster for Mobutu. The MPLA was safely installed in Luanda, surrounded by Cuban troops. Mobutu was a dirty word in the world of African nationalism. The CIA's involvement, once public, ensured that the next American president would be less willing to respond to Mobutu's hysterics over

MPLA troops, trained by Cubans, pass in review

Communist advances as it generated a storm of controversy in the U.S. Congress. The FAZ had once again demonstrated its impotence. Most important, Neto owed the FNLC a favor for its support in the war, a favor that might include support for an FNLC attempt to retake its old territory, now called Shaba. The ex-gendarmes would not wait long to demand their payment.

III. SHABA I

On 8 March 1977, the FNLC, under the command of General Nathaniel Mbumba, invaded Zaire's Shaba province from Angola. Approximately 2,000 men on bicycles crossed the Zairian border. Their drive met virtually no resistance as they proceeded along the railroad that crossed the border at Dilolo, divided into columns, and headed for different objectives throughout the province (see map 2). At 1330, one FNLC company occupied the manganese mining town of Kisenge, killing the FAZ squad leader charged with its defense. The remainder of the squad escaped to Malonga to report the invasion. Mobutu's eighty-day war had begun.[1]

The FNLC units rapidly seized their initial objectives. Reports came in that Kapanga was in rebel hands by 1430 on the 8th. On 9 March, Dilolo fell to rebel control, followed by Kasaji and Mutshatsha on the 10th. By 15 March, the rebels held Sandoa. The Zairian response to the invasion was sluggish and uncoordinated even though, in 1976, reports had arrived from the province indicating that the FNLC was actively recruiting young men of military age among the Lunda. In addition, in March 1977, additional reports claimed that the FNLC had plans to invade. Such reports were ignored and, in some cases, actively discouraged. A division of troops protected the area, but as a tension-reducing measure, Mobutu had ordered that the border remain free of large units. When the FNLC moved, those units near the invasion area failed to act decisively. Though Mobutu dispatched Colonel Mampa Ngakwe Salamayi, the army chief of staff, to take command of the operations center in Kolwezi on 9 March, the FAZ reaction to the invasion remained dismal. On the 10th, two companies of the 2d Airborne Battalion moving from Kasaji to Divuma ran into an ambush near Malonga. Suffering only one killed, the 93-man force fled and abandoned all crew-served weapons, including heavy machine guns, a 75-mm cannon, and mortars.[2]

To reinforce the region, the FAZ headquarters in Kinshasa ordered the 11th Brigade of the newly formed Kaymanyola Division flown to Shaba. Intended to be an elite unit, the Kaymanyola Division was a new concept for the FAZ. Activated under North Korean instructors, the unit was a melting pot of all tribes and walks of life in Zairian society, an attempt to reduce tribal influence and hatreds within the FAZ. Unfortunately, the Kaymanyola Division had been in existence only six months when it was ordered into battle. Two of the 11th Brigade battalions arrived in Kolwezi on the 12th and were immediately committed with the remainder of the 2d Airborne

17

18

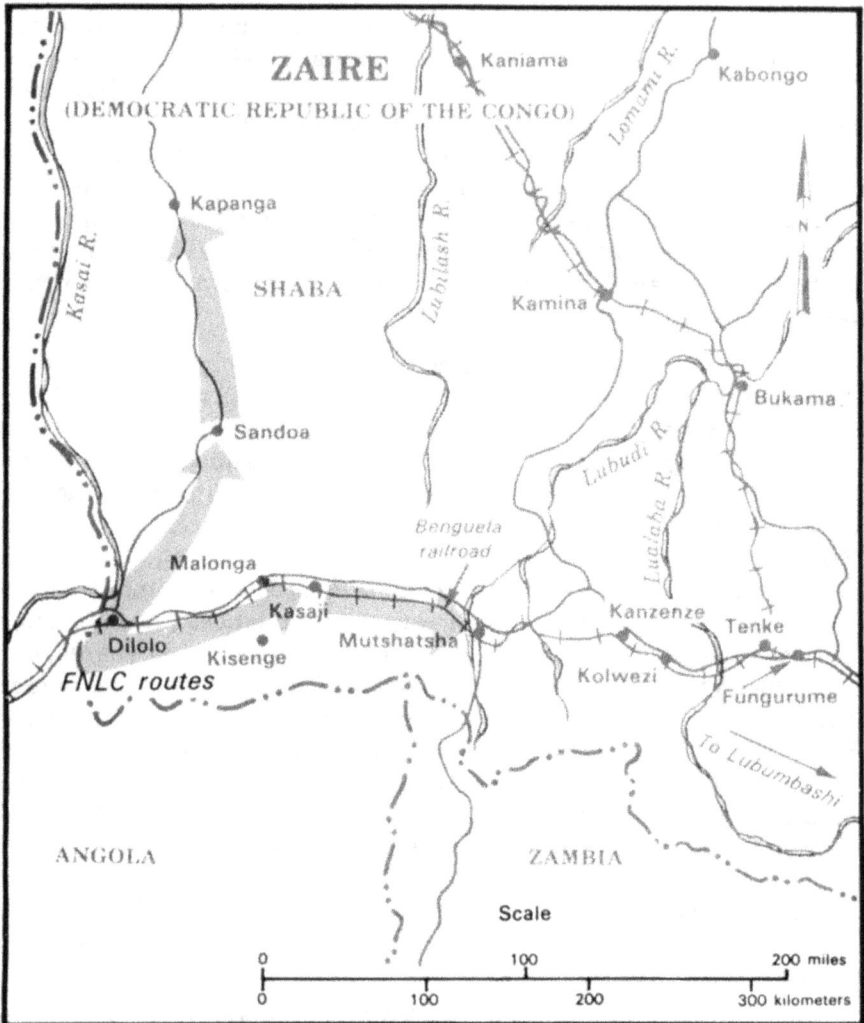

Map 2. The FNLC's first invasion into Shaba, March 1977

Battalion. Under the command of Lieutenant Colonel Monkoti, the composite unit fell apart as soon as it made contact with the FNLC, requiring two days to reorganize. Finally, on the 18th, Monkoti led the force in a march on Kasaji. Once again, the FNLC ambushed the unit, but this time, it held together, sustaining two dead, two missing, and three wounded, while killing fifteen of the FNLC. Meanwhile, the remaining units of the division were still in Kinshasa awaiting transportation to the war zone.[3]

Confusion prevailed at the regional headquarters, and Mobutu began to involve himself directly. The FAZ regional headquarters ordered the 3d Company of the 4th Battalion, a Kinshasa-based unit on temporary duty in Kolwezi, to reinforce Sandoa. Arriving in the town, the unit commander, Lieutenant Munganga, took his unit back to Kolwezi, leaving the town to be occupied by the FNLC the next day. Such withdrawals and the initial defeats suffered by the 2d Airborne and the Kaymanyola Division angered Mobutu, and he relieved Colonel Salamayi six days after the unfortunate colonel had taken command. On the 23d, Mobutu relieved Salamayi's replacement, along with all the staff in Kolwezi.[4]

The situation remained grim for the FAZ. Due to morale problems, Monkoti's force was out of combat by the 23d. A company of commandos under Major Tshibangu arrived in Kolwezi on the 23d. Sent to Mutshatsha on the 24th along with Monkoti's unit, the two units fought isolated engagements the next day. On the 27th, a company of pygmies commanded by Lieutenant Colonel Mukobo reinforced Tshibangu at Mutshatsha, and both units conducted uncoordinated counterattacks that failed. Their only success was that they managed to link up in time to withdraw.[5]

Once again, the FAZ moved to stop the invasion through reorganization. The FAZ headquarters in Kamina divided the operational area into three zones centering on Kamina, Kolwezi, and Luiza. That, however, did not placate Mobutu, who on the 29th again changed operational commanders, this time placing Brigadier General Singa Boyenge Mosambay in command. Singa received more reinforcements as the 12th Brigade of the Kaymanyola Division moved by rail from Kamina to Kolwezi at the end of the month. Another force, two battalions of the airborne division under Colonel Songambele, arrived at Kamina with orders to deploy to Kanzenze, sixty kilometers from Kolwezi. Songambele put his headquarters there as directed but deployed his units 139 kilometers the other side of Kolwezi. To avoid confusion, the local air commander refused to allow aircraft to fly resupply missions unless he personally approved each one. In summary, the first month of Shaba I was a disaster for the FAZ. On 7 April, however, things began to look better, for a French liaison party arrived to coordinate the deployment of Moroccan troops to Zaire. Thus, a decade after the FAZ had claimed victory over the Katangans, it once again needed foreign assistance to fight its old foe.[6]

For Mobutu, the attack should not have come as a surprise. In compliance with the Brazzaville Accords, Mobutu had ceased supporting the FNLA and had many of its camps withdrawn from the

Zairian troops prepare for battle near the Angolan border in Shaba.
Note the Moroccan adviser (wearing the beret).

border. But he had increased his support of UNITA, and he continued support to FLEC (Front for the Liberation of the Cabinda Enclave) incursions into Cabinda. In Brazzaville, Neto and Mobutu had agreed to normalize relations, but this relationship had proved to be a short-lived honeymoon. Angered by Zaire's continued support of his enemies, Neto claimed that the FAZ was once more preparing to invade Angola. Meanwhile, the leadership of the FNLC established links with other dissident groups as it prepared for the invasion.[7]

Certainly, numerous groups were willing to discuss Mobutu's ouster. By one count, some thirty-two gathered in Paris to build support for the invasion. Some of these dissident organizations agreed to provide men for the invasion. Reportedly, the People's Liberation Party from Kivu, famous for the kidnapping of Jane Goodall's three assistants in 1975, and the Democratic Force for the Liberation of the

Congo, led by Antoine Gizenga of the abortive Stanleyville regime, provided troops and supplies.[8]

In any case, Neto provided the most important support for the FNLC. In return for that sponsorship, the FNLC mined and patrolled UNITA infiltration routes into Angola. While Neto reportedly was growing tired of the FNLC's free reign in eastern Angola, Mobutu's clumsy support for Angolan insurgent groups ensured that the Angolan leader would provide the logistical base for the invasion. Mobutu could only blame himself.[9]

As the invasion proceeded apace, Mobutu demonstrated little inclination toward self-criticism. Very quickly, he seized on the ties between the FNLC and the Cubans in Angola to generate the idea that this was a Communist invasion. Appeals to the Organization of African Unity (OAU) on this basis made little progress, but the

Zairian troops at an assembly area in southern Shaba

invasion had broken two African rules of acceptability: the FNLC had crossed international borders, and more important, the FNLC, heavily Lunda based, appeared to be launching a tribal attack. Nothing makes African leaders more nervous than cross-border tribal unrest. In a grand gesture of solidarity, Idi Amin flew to Zaire and offered the unspecified services of his "suicide squad"; other African nations also voiced support for the oft-criticized Mobutu. Yet none seemed overly impressed by his version of a Communist threat. So while the OAU spoke against the invasion, the international body failed to react to cries of Cuban activity.[10]

The OAU was not alone in this indifference to the Cuban threat. Mobutu next turned to the United States for assistance. Long a supporter of Mobutu, the United States had been a principal supplier of military aid, donating around $400 million in aid since the early 1960s. Moreover, the United States had underwritten much of the United Nations' expense in stabilizing the Congo and had funded the CIA's Congolese version of Air America, with its exiled Cuban pilots, during the Simba Rebellion. Also, the U.S. Air Force had flown the airlift operations that helped put down the 1967 mercenary revolt.

Idi Amin with Mobutu

President Jimmy Carter's administration did not provide the support Mobutu had hoped for

More recently, the CIA had funded the FNLA's struggle against the Cubans in Angola. Now, the Cubans were back—this time, however, they were on the wrong side of the border. Surely, Mobutu could count on the Americans to help him against a Cuban invasion.[11]

In 1977 in Washington, D.C., nothing could have been less likely. President Jimmy Carter and his administration were not known for their support of the controversial Mobutu. Instead, the administration leaned toward Nigeria, Zaire's rival, as the key player in African politics. In general, the Carter administration at this stage regarded Africa's problems as regional and therefore subject to regional solutions. Since détente was not yet on the shoals, Carter and his aides, save National Security Adviser Zbigniew Brzezinski, were more concerned with preserving the status quo. Andrew Young, the U.S. ambassador to the United Nations, publicly dismissed the danger of Marxist Africa and gibed at Mobutu's inability to handle the FNLC. Moreover, in view of its emphasis on human rights, the Carter administration could hardly be expected to rally behind Mobutu's regime, of which the State Department had once said, "Generally, after interrogation, nonpolitical prisoners are not subject to repeated beatings."[12]

Suffice it to say, Mobutu received less support in Washington than he had hoped. Aside from a statement by the State Department that the situation was "dangerous," little anti-Communist hysteria

24

National Security Adviser Zbigniew Brzezinski

Department of State

crept into the administration's response. Agreeing to speed up the delivery of military assistance materiel that Washington quickly described as nonlethal, the United States chartered civilian DC-8s to airlift the supplies. As the crisis continued, Congress actually reduced credits for military assistance from $30 to $15 million—so much for U.S. support in the Shaba I affair.[13]

Mobutu next approached Brussels, and as in the case of the United States, he came away disappointed. As his initial request, Mobutu asked for 1,000 paras, a bid for support that drew little serious consideration from the Belgians. In consideration of the safety of their nationals in the war zone, the Belgians were unlikely to intervene to support the FAZ. Furthermore, with an approaching election, the time was hardly ripe for new Belgian adventures in Zaire. Besides, the Belgian business community had hardly forgiven Mobutu for his nationalization programs of 1973 and 1974. Aside from additional supplies of small arms and crew-served weapons, Mobutu received little else from his ex-patrons.[14]

Just as things were looking bleak for obtaining outside military assistance, Mobutu received help from unexpected quarters. A traditional Muslim and rabid anti-Communist, King Hassan of Morocco offered the services of a combat-experienced paratroop brigade. Matching Morocco's support, Egypt agreed to provide a group of trained pilots and mechanics to back up Mobutu's limited air force.

Ambassador Andrew Young gibed
at Mobutu's inability to handle the
FNLC

Finally, Saudi Arabia granted funds to defray the operation. Under the command of two colonels who had served in the UN force in the Congo, the force was to fight alongside the FAZ if airlift could be arranged.[15]

In a move that rankled Belgian sensitivities, France agreed to provide the airlift needed by the Moroccans. President Giscard d'Estaing ordered the action without consulting France's National Assembly. Reportedly bowing to pressure from francophone Africa to contain Soviet-Cuban advances on the continent, d'Estaing already knew the request was coming. Colonel Yves Gras, head of the French Military Mission (MMF) in Zaire, was responsible for the foreign intervention to rescue Mobutu.[16]

Gras, with thirty-seven years of service, was an experienced soldier. After leaving Saint-Cyr in 1941, he had taken part in a revolt of the cadets after the Italian occupation of Aix-en-Provence in November 1942. Later, the determined Frenchman escaped through Spain to Morocco where he joined the French colonial forces to fight in Italy and France. After recovering from wounds received in the liberation of his homeland, Gras went overseas again, seeing active service in Madagascar, Indochina, and Algeria. By the time of his posting to Zaire in 1976, he had developed a reputation for directness that was respected if not always welcomed. Fortunately for Gras, his ambassador in Zaire was of a similar mold.[17]

Morocco's King Hassan

Africa Report

André Ross, after thirty years in the French diplomatic service, was a respected and experienced ambassador. He, too, was also known for a willingness to speak his mind. More important, Ross worked well with his military colleagues. As the initial drama of Shaba I unfolded, he dispatched Gras to the area to study the situation. When Gras reported that a battalion of French paras could regain the upper hand but that unaided the FAZ could not throw out the FNLC, Ross agreed but said that the affair would be better left to an African country. Ross' political officer, Ivan Bastouil, suggested Morocco, a suggestion that was ultimately accepted by the governments of France, Morocco, and Zaire.[18]

In addition to orchestrating the Moroccan involvement, France provided direct assistance to the FAZ. Already Zaire's principal arms dealer, France provided the FAZ with Mirage fighters, Panhard armored cars, and Puma helicopters. After employing eleven military aircraft to fly in the Moroccans, France provided additional arms, ammunition, and a twenty-man team from SDECE, the French external security service, to help coordinate Shaba's defensive plans.[19]

France's purpose in acting so decisively to aid Zaire was consonant with its activist policy toward the African continent. Even after the collapse of the struggle for Algeria, France had maintained strong commitments to support francophone countries in Africa.

French President
Valéry Giscard d'Estaing

France had troops stationed in the Ivory Coast, Djibouti, Senegal, and Gabon. At the time of Shaba I, the French Foreign Legion was engaged in Chad. In short, France, and President d'Estaing in particular, took a strong interest in African affairs. Considering the relative importance of Africa's resources to European industry, such concern was understandable.[20]

Zaire supplied nearly 80 percent of its exports to Europe and drew 67 percent of its imports from European markets. D'Estaing had visited Kinshasa in 1975 at a time when Mobutu's stature needed a boost. For this gesture, French business won a $500 million contract for telecommunications equipment. The company that won the Zairian contract was Thomson CSF International under financing provided by the Banque Francaise du Commerce Extérieur. Both the company and the bank were headed by members of d'Estaing's family. Still, France's total investment in Zaire was only $20 million, compared to the estimated $750 million to $1 billion from Belgium and the $200 million from the United States. So, the intervention offered France an opportunity to pursue economic interests at the same time that it supported its self-proclaimed role as Africa's guardian. Consequently, as Mobutu and the FAZ breathed a collective sigh of relief at the arrival of the French liaison team in Kolwezi, Belgian eyebrows rose in suspicion at the rapidity and extent of the French response to the beleaguered Zairian's plea for help.[21]

The arrival of the Moroccans on 9 April dramatically changed the course of the war. Only some sixty kilometers from Kolwezi, the FNLC's attack had permanently stalled, and now, the FAZ and Moroccans prepared to drive the FNLC out. The combined headquarters at Kolwezi launched a two-pronged attack by moving two brigades on parallel axes toward Dilolo and Sandoa. Backed by the Moroccans and supported by air strikes, artillery, and armor, the attack kicked off on 13 April. After an inauspicious beginning—the lead FAZ unit retreated almost twenty kilometers after receiving fire—the attack proceeded in fits and starts. Over the remainder of April and most of May, the FAZ, with the Moroccans in trail, gradually prodded the FNLC westward along the railroad and back into Angola. On 28 May, Mobutu claimed victory over the invaders. His eighty-day war was over, but the trouble in Shaba was only beginning.[22]

Shaba I was hardly over before its repercussions began. The people of the province were the first to suffer a repeat of the 1967 reprisals. As soon as the last of the FNLC had crossed the border, the FAZ turned on the local population, with the most savage reprisals falling on the heads of the Lunda. Although the FNLC had announced that it sought to overthrow Mobutu by seizing Shaba, the local population had remained aloof from the campaign. Their caution, however, failed to protect them, and within the coming months, over 200,000 slipped across the border into Angola to escape FAZ vengeance.[23]

As for the FAZ, its ultimate success on the battlefield did not save it from Mobutu's vengeance. Numerous officers were purged and brought to trial for complicity in the invasion, cowardice, or incompetence. Among those dismissed were Ngunza Karl I. Bond, the chief of staff of the FAZ; his adviser, Bizeni-Mana; Munguya-Mbenge, the former Shaba province commissioner; the chief of the Lunda; and Colonel Mampa Ngua, the chief of staff of the FAZ ground forces. By March 1978, the wheels of Zairian justice began to roll in the trial of ninety-one defendants, twenty-four civilians, and sixty-seven military officers. Penalties were severe: nineteen death sentences, of which thirteen were executed, and prison sentences ranging from five to twenty years.[24]

During this round of trials and executions, the FAZ was completely reorganized. Reduced in strength by 25 percent, the units were streamlined and reequipped by drawing on recent foreign

Mobutu assumed control of military operations

military aid. The "elite" Kaymanyola Division established its headquarters in Kolwezi, and at the recommendation of Colonel Gras, the MMF began training an entirely new airborne unit. The efforts of the MMF, its U.S. counterpart, the U.S. Military Assistance Mission in Zaire (ZAMISH), and their Belgian associates focused on producing a FAZ that could at least defend itself against the FNLC.[25]

Unfortunately for the FAZ, the FNLC remained a viable force. Moreover, it could legitimately regard itself as undefeated, as it had withdrawn from Shaba at its own pace. With the FAZ's actions in Shaba after the war, the FNLC gained in strength. When it crossed into Zaire, it had boasted at most 2,000 armed men. After the war, it enrolled approximately 5,000 soldiers who looked forward to another round with Mobutu. Besides the recruitment of new members, the FNLC left behind a number of men who were able to lose themselves in the local population. Based on its growing support, the FNLC's leadership realized that in the next campaign it would be able to seize Kolwezi, a move that might topple Mobutu.[26]

While Mobutu's popularity had been at one of its lowest points before the war, his victory had made him a hero. When the war broke out, Mobutu's standing had plummeted in Kinshasa, but his flamboyance in assuming command and the foreign aid that had come to him reversed the trend. In cultivating both local and foreign support, he promised needed reforms in all areas of Zairian life. Following the campaign, he used the purge trials of the FAZ and government as showcases to prove he was taking the actions promised. By November, Mobutu easily won a vote of confidence extending his rule another seven years.[27]

Even as he rebuilt domestic support, Mobutu restored foreign confidence in his ability to govern Zaire. Of course, France remained firmly behind the Zairian strongman. A real surprise came with the outspoken support of the People's Republic of China, as the Chinese took advantage of the situation to lambaste the Soviets in the United Nations. The Carter administration, after its chilly response to requests for increased military aid during the war, increased military aid to the Zairians. Even Belgium attempted to restore some warmth to its relations with Mobutu by expelling a dissident leader believed to have been involved in the invasion.[28]

However well things might have been going for Mobutu in Zaire and with the West, his relations with Neto still remained hostile. Regardless of Neto's difficulties in controlling the activities of the FNLC or his desire to rid himself of them and over 200,000 refugees, he could not countenance Mobutu's continued support for UNITA. The Angolan leader soon found it easier to allow the FNLC to resume its operations against Mobutu.[29]

IV. SHABA II BEGINS

Shortly after midnight on 11 May 1978, 3,000 to 4,000 members of the FNLC slipped quietly into Zaire from Zambia. Organized into 11 "battalions," each with about 300 men, the force divided into 2 groups and pushed on in the darkness. One group of around 1,000 men headed toward the town of Mutshatsha to cut the railroad. The second had a more important mission: to seize the city of Kolwezi (see map 3).[1]

The FNLC's route was well prepared. After the reprisals taken by the FAZ against the locals for their support of the 1977 invasion, the FNLC had found it easy to infiltrate the province in strength over the previous six months. These infiltrators, along with stay-behind elements, had busily recruited among the locals, particularly among the Lunda around Kolwezi. There, the FNLC had recruited some 500 young men and organized them into a local militia. Now, these locals guided the FNLC into hiding positions around the targets. Breaking open weapon caches smuggled in on charcoal trucks from Zambia, the FNLC distributed arms and ammunition to the local recruits. The final touch was to ensure that each recruit wore the FNLC's tiger armband, which helped with identification. Preparations completed, the rebels rested and waited through the following day, a day of unusually high absenteeism among the local GECAMINES employees.[2]

Operation Colombe was going exactly as planned. This time, General Mbumba's forces were not going to squander their efforts on unimportant villages. By seizing the mining capital of Kolwezi, the FNLC would take Zaire and Mobutu by the throat. Following the fall of Kolwezi, the next targets were to be Likasi and Lubumbashi. Mbumba's goal was no less than the ouster of Mobutu, and the disruption of the mining industry was to be the key to his removal. In choosing to infiltrate through areas of Zambia populated by the Lunda, the FNLC had avoided the strength of the FAZ. With over 8,000 troops in Shaba, the FAZ felt that it could control the Angolan border. But the FAZ had left Kolwezi and the border with Zambia virtually unguarded.[3]

At first light on 13 May, the FNLC struck Kolwezi. Unfortunately for the city's inhabitants, the invaders were up against the Kaymanyola Division's 14th Brigade, considered by FAZ headquarters as the weakest unit in the division. Ironically, with the Kaymanyola's other brigades aligned along the Angola border, FAZ headquarters had stationed the 14th Brigade in Kolwezi along the "safe" border with Zambia. Consequently, while many FAZ soldiers fought valiantly

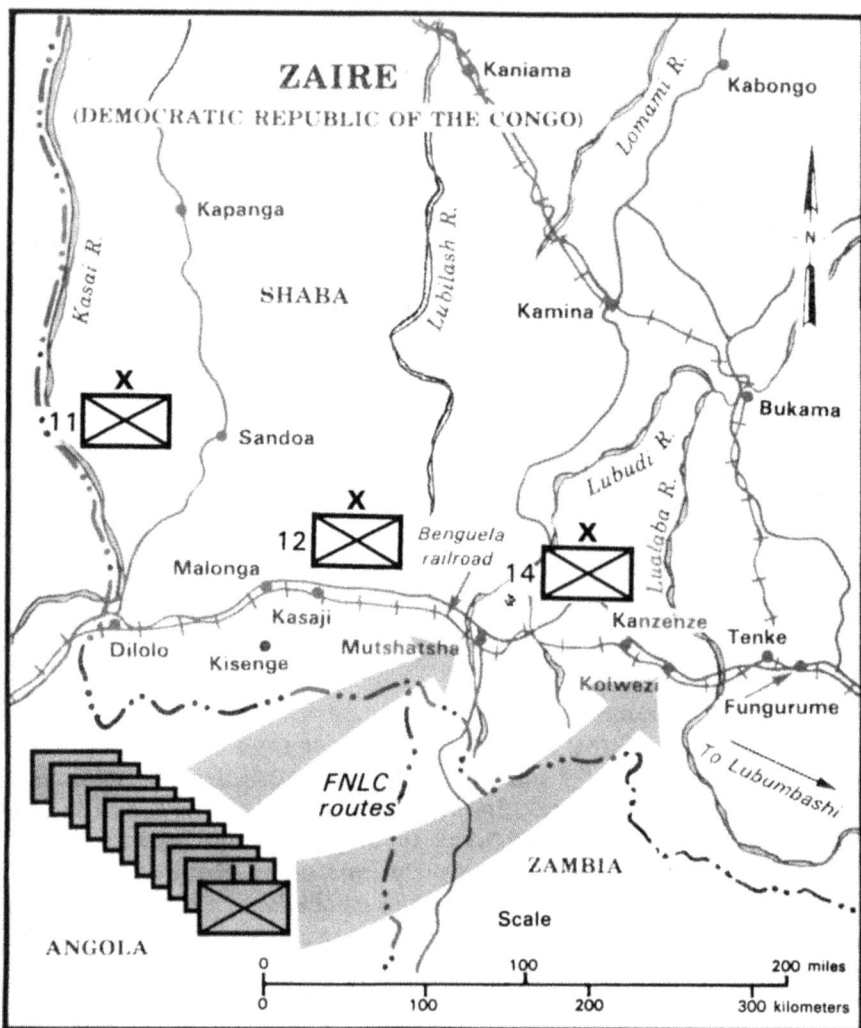

Map 3. The FNLC's second invasion into Shaba, May 1978

against the FNLC's attack, the 14th Brigade rapidly fell apart. Quickly overrunning the airfield, the rebels destroyed all FAZ aircraft on the field: five to seven Italian Macchi ground attack aircraft, two to four Cessna 310s, a Buffalo transport, and two helicopters. Brigadier Tshiveka, the commander, disappeared and was not heard from until he surfaced at Tenke-Fungurume days later. By 1000, the FNLC controlled the airport, the FAZ depots, and most of the town. FAZ survivors had three choices: attempt to hide, hold out until reinforcements arrived, or surrender and join the FNLC. No alternative guaranteed survival.[4]

For the foreigners, 13 May was not to be the lazy Saturday most had planned. At 0500, Henry Jagodinski, a 46-year-old worker for GECAMINES, woke to the sound of barking dogs. Failing to go back to sleep, Jagodinski and his Chokwe wife, Angeline, began to prepare breakfast. Soon, both heard firing around the town. Jagodinski passed it off as the usual FAZ activity, an assumption soon disproved by running gun battles outside between the FAZ and unidentified troops. Though the fighting quickly passed by, the Jagodinskis were joined at breakfast by an FNLC search party. After questioning them on weapons or FAZ survivors, the FNLC soldiers ate and departed.[5]

Across town, the situation was more sensitive. In their home, Maurice and Maryse Faverjon, a French couple, listened to rounds slam into the walls. Maurice was surprised. A veteran of Shaba I, he had never felt any danger and had just sent for Maryse in January. The previous evening, his houseboy had warned them that a new war would soon start. Faverjon had dismissed the warning with a laugh; however, he was not laughing now. By telephone, Faverjon learned that the French military advisers and several Moroccans had been shot. Rumors abounded: an American had been shot as a mercenary, Cuban advisers were running the operation, and FNLC soldiers were searching all the homes. Just then, Faverjon became very frightened as an FNLC soldier arrived and demanded to see Faverjon's son. After identifying himself as the son of a former house servant, the rebel assured the Faverjons that they would not be harmed.[6]

Although most of the foreign population was not in immediate danger, some individuals were at risk. The rumor that the French advisers had been shot out of hand proved to be untrue, but Lieutenant Jacques Laissac; Chief Adjutant Pierre Nuvel; and Adjutants Jacques Bireau, Jacques Gomilla, Bernard Laurent, and Christian Cesario had disappeared under FNLC control. They never returned. The FNLC had come prepared with lists of people subject to trial by the "People's Court of Justice," and that tribunal was soon in session. Conviction by the drumhead court carried an almost guaranteed death sentence. In the expatriate community, the French and anyone who appeared to be Moroccan were in danger of being arrested. As for the local population, those reported to be loyal to Kinshasa soon found themselves behind bars—if they were lucky.[7]

Initially, the FNLC was remarkably disciplined and certainly better behaved than the FAZ. The danger from random violence came from two other sources. The first was from the FAZ, who continued to fight around the regional headquarters in the new town, or from scattered survivors in hiding around the city, most of whom had gone to ground in the European quarters rather than in the hostile native sections. The second came from the FNLC's local recruits who, like the jeunesse of the Simba Rebellion, harbored grudges against the affluence of their European neighbors. The presence of FAZ deserters eager to prove their enthusiasm for the new regime added to the precariousness of the situation. That instability held the potential for extreme violence, violence that Kinshasa could do little to halt.[8]

First word of the invasion came from a Belgian pilot attempting to land at the Kolwezi airfield. His plane was hit by small-arms fire, and the surprised Belgian flew on to Lubumbashi to relay the news. By 1000, in Kinshasa, the news of the attack had reached Western embassies.[9]

André Ross, the French ambassador, had just returned from the airport where he and most of the other ambassadors had waited all morning to depart on a Mobutu-sponsored trip to Boende. Finally, Mobutu's staff, without giving a reason, had relayed word that the trip was canceled. At 1000, Ross learned from Colonel Larzul, the military attaché, that the Kolwezi airfield had been attacked and most of its aircraft destroyed. Almost simultaneously, Colonel Gras, commander of the MMF, one floor above Ross' office, received a telex from Lubumbashi reporting the invasion. Even as Gras read the cable, Ross called him downstairs.[10]

Of the three men gathered in Ross' office, none was surprised by the invasion, only by its timing. In April, Ross had submitted a report to Paris on the current state of affairs in preparation for the upcoming French-African conference. He had referred to Shaba as an occupied territory rather than an integral part of Zaire, and he thought a new attack was probable. In assessing the capability of the FAZ to defend the area, Ross relied on Larzul, who bitingly referred to the FAZ as "le grande corps invertébré [the great spineless body]." Neither Larzul nor Gras believed the FAZ had recovered from its disastrous showing the previous year. What had hindered their ability to predict the present attack was an action taken by Mobutu. In his purge of FAZ headquarters, Mobutu had fired a Belgian major named Van Melle who had worked in the FAZ intelligence directorate. Van Melle had routinely passed intelligence to the Western embassies in Kinshasa, but his Zairian replacement was hardly as cooperative.[11]

Ross needed additional information, and the three split up to gather it. Larzul went directly to FAZ headquarters, where he met with General Babia, the chief of staff. Babia confirmed the news from Kolwezi and reported that the rebels had infiltrated through Zambia. Nevertheless, Babia claimed that the FAZ's 1st Military Region headquarters and the 14th Brigade remained in contact by radio and in control of the situation. Meanwhile, Gras conferred with his own contacts at the headquarters who, with a few bribes, related the same story given to Larzul. Concurrently, Ross visited the Belgian and the American Embassies to consult with his counterparts, who also confirmed earlier reports.[12]

Comparing notes back in the French Embassy, Ross, Larzul, and Gras prepared to notify Paris of the Shaba invasion. It had been Ross' nightmare of the previous year that the FNLC would take Kolwezi with its 2,500 Europeans, 400 of whom were French. Now, a little more than fourteen months later, the nightmare had come true. With the situation confused and the status of the FAZ unclear, Ross cabled Paris that an attack on Kolwezi had occurred and the expatriate population remained in the city. The message reached Paris at 131305 May 1978.[13]

Shortly after the first message had been dispatched, Gras received further intelligence. The GECAMINES headquarters in Lubumbashi had been able to maintain telephone contact with its people in Kolwezi. These contacts reported that the FNLC, wearing the tiger emblem it wore the previous year and armed with AK-47s, had control of the city. Happily, the reports indicated that the FNLC had behaved well toward the expatriates. Other information identified an FNLC column headed toward Mutshatsha. Gras quickly grasped that this was not simply a raid but a major operation to seize Shaba. The FNLC had already succeeded on the first day of this invasion in doing what it had failed to do throughout the 1977 invasion. Again, Ross fired off a cable to Paris, and the three Frenchmen headed for FAZ headquarters once more.[14]

Arriving there, Ross noticed that most of the senior diplomats in the city were also on hand. Significantly, Mobutu was present and in uniform. Never hesitant to dramatize events, Mobutu announced that Kolwezi had been attacked by light units of the FNLC. This his audience already knew, but Mobutu stunned his audience when he added that the FAZ had known in advance that the FNLC was planning an attack. Operation Colombe, Mobutu claimed, was a Cuban-supported attack to seize the towns of Kolwezi, Mutshatsha, and Lubumbashi. Mobutu further announced that he had intended to disclose the plan on 20 May before its scheduled execution date of 1 June. Asking to be excused, Mobutu waited as the other diplomats left and pulled Ross aside to tell him that he had personally warned the Soviet ambassador that the U.S.S.R. must stop the invasion. Once again, the French ambassador returned to his office to inform Paris.[15]

While Ross was meeting with Mobutu, the ambassador's two military advisers were interviewing General Babia. Gras and Larzul wanted to know the status of the FAZ headquarters in Kolwezi. Both knew Babia had ordered the 133d Infantry Battalion and the 311th Airborne Battalion to be placed on alert. The 311th had formed six months earlier under the tutelage of French advisers commanded by Lieutenant Colonel Ballade, who had informed Gras, his commander, as soon as the alert order came down. Had Babia been planning something? Far from mounting a hasty operation, Babia seemed absolutely confident that the FAZ had the Shaba crisis under control.[16]

Any such thought was absolute fantasy. Gras, Larzul, and Ross knew the capacity of the FAZ to fabricate victory out of defeat. The victory parades following Shaba I were prime examples. But without a Zairian call for assistance, neither the French nor any other power could act. President d'Estaing had gone so far as to telephone Mobutu. Though thanked for his solicitude, d'Estaing received no request for assistance. In fact, Mobutu repeated Babia's assurances that the FAZ had everything under control.[17]

For the Jagodinski family, the events of 14 May left little doubt as to who had control of Kolwezi. After spending the night sleeping in their central hallway to avoid stray bullets, the Jagodinskis were awakened by pounding on their door. Henry answered the door and found a young and thoroughly drugged rebel soldier demanding to see their passports. Angeline found the documents, but it was obvious the soldier could not read them. Still, he appeared satisfied, until he started to leave and spotted a wounded FAZ soldier hiding in a ditch beside the house. Yelling threats in Swahili, he covered the Jagodinskis with his weapon and was ready to fire when one of their children ran forward to greet him. The presence of the child defused the situation, and the soldier left, prodding his FAZ prisoner in front of him. Encountering members of an FNLC patrol just down the street, he called them over, and they promptly shot the prisoner. Later, the FNLC soldiers returned and searched the area more thoroughly. Finding another FAZ soldier, they beat him senseless and put a bullet through his head. Clearly, the FAZ was not in control.[18]

By the end of the 14th, the expatriates in Kolwezi knew that they, too, were in mortal danger. That afternoon, following the murder of the second prisoner, the Jagodinskis saw their neighbor, Mr. Marreckx, led off by an FNLC patrol. His crime, one that cost him his life, was the possession of a military-style riding jacket. A similar piece of clothing almost proved fatal to Maryse Faverjon. That morning, she wore an olive-drab blouse styled with epaulets. An FNLC soldier spotted her from the street and opened fire, thinking she was a mercenary. Reinforced by more soldiers, the FNLC unit searched the house and threatened to take away her husband since the mercenary seen earlier could not be found. In two other incidents, the FNLC arrested European men and went through mock trials, followed by mock firing squads. Both were released, but they saw evidence that convinced them that most of the firing squads were real.[19]

Back in Kinshasa, the day had started early at the French Embassy. Ross and his military advisers met to review the situation. Ross had been in contact with the Belgian and U.S. Embassies, both of which had direct communications with GECAMINES in Lubumbashi. Summarizing their reports, Ross pointed out that, so far, the FNLC had shown no hostility toward Europeans and had maintained discipline. They were a uniformed, well-led, and reasonably well-armed force. Beyond that bit of intelligence, nothing else had developed.[20]

For Gras, the situation was clearly dangerous enough to warrant action. He was convinced the attack was an invasion, and he knew from the previous year that the FAZ could not handle the invasion with its units in Shaba. Backed by Larzul, Gras convinced Ross of the threat to the expatriates in Kolwezi. Determined to force a response from Paris, Ross telephoned the Élysée, the French president's residence.[21]

Ross spoke to Colonel Mermet, who was on duty at the residence. Mermet assured Ross that President d'Estaing had read all the messages on Shaba and was personally involved. Ross then went on the offensive, warning that 3,000 Europeans should be considered hostages. He further warned that, as evidenced by the news of a secondary attack on Mutshatsha, the attack on Kolwezi was only part of a larger operation to seize all of Shaba. Ross then turned the telephone over to Gras, who promptly asked that two companies of French paratroops be sent to reinforce the FAZ. Gras explained that he intended to reinforce the 311th Airborne Battalion in order to conduct an airborne assault on Kolwezi. He also requested that the French advisers under Lieutenant Colonel Ballade be allowed to serve with the unit on the proposed operation. Ending the call, Ross and Gras sat back and waited for a response.[22]

As one might expect when a colonel calls Paris asking for troops to intervene in central Africa, a positive response would not be immediate. René Journiac, President d'Estaing's adviser on African affairs, was against a unilateral intervention at this stage. D'Estaing was, in any case, waiting for the Zairians to request assistance formally. Further, both d'Estaing and Journiac felt it imperative that the Belgians take the initiative in this crisis. Only in an extreme situation would Paris consider a military intervention, and then it would have to be a combined Belgian-French operation.[23]

While the Belgian initiative never materialized, the Zairian request was only minutes from delivery. Shortly after Ross had finished speaking with Paris, the Zairian Ministry of Foreign Affairs called requesting Ross' presence at an important meeting. Ross hurried to the presidential residence where Foreign Minister Idzumbuir announced to an audience of ambassadors, which did not include the Soviet representative, that Zaire was making a formal request for "aide de toute nature [aid of every nature]." Appearing in fatigues to enhance the drama, Mobutu entered and repeated his minister's request. Ross now had the request demanded by Paris, but he still needed to know how the Belgians planned to react.[24]

As Ross hurried back to the embassy, Gras met with General Babia, who no longer appeared confident that the FAZ could contain the situation in Shaba. The attack on Mutshatsha had contradicted his earlier dismissal of the invasion as a mere raid on Kolwezi. Never one to hesitate, Gras urged Babia to airlift the 311th Airborne and 133d Infantry Battalions to Lubumbashi using the FAZ's C-130s and Air Zaire's DC-10 and DC-8. Gras also recommended that the cadets at the military academy be converted to an infantry battalion and sent to join the 311th and 133d. Once assembled, the units were to launch a drive to seize the Lualaba bridge, some forty kilometers from Kolwezi. Such a move would cover the approach to Likasi and facilitate a future move to regain Kolwezi. Gras was successful. By evening, the 133d was in Lubumbashi, and the 311th was on standby to move. Satisfied that he had convinced Babia to take the initiative, Gras returned to brief Ross.[25]

At the embassy, Ross was listening to another briefing, this one from the irate Larzul. Following his return from the Ministry of Foreign Affairs, Ross had sent Larzul to the Belgian Embassy to sound out the Belgians on their position on military intervention. Larzul returned within the hour angry and disappointed. The Belgians felt the situation did not warrant a military response. Instead, they were in contact with the FNLC representatives in Brussels and were attempting to negotiate a release of the European population. Failing that, military intervention would be used only as a last resort, and it would be conducted along the lines of the Stanleyville rescue. Though Larzul was disappointed at this stage of the conversation, he had no reason to become angry until his Belgian counterpart continued, "I must assure you that a French intervention would be considered by us as inopportune and unfriendly." Gras, back at the embassy in time to hear Larzul's response, became more convinced that the French were going to have to act. Whether it would be a combined operation with the FAZ as he had proposed to Paris, he could not say. However, he could see that if Paris waited for Brussels to respond, the response might come too late.[26]

By Monday, 15 May, the world's attention was focused on Shaba province. In Washington, Brussels, and Paris, crisis committees were studying the situation. For the United States, beyond a Zairian priority request for military assistance supplies, the major concern was the eighty-odd Americans located in or near Kolwezi. As the U.S. Embassy and its consulate in Lubumbashi painstakingly went over the lists of Americans in the area, they set the number at eighty-nine. Most of the Americans were in a construction camp eight kilometers north of the city. The company, Morris-Knudsen, had a contract to work on the Inga-Shaba power line project and was equipped with its own aircraft. With two DC-3s, one Piper Aztec, and two Bell 206 helicopters, the company was already considering an air evacuation of the seventy-four people in the camp. That still left an estimated fifteen Americans in the area. In a dramatic shift from the yawning response of the Carter administration the year before, the request for U.S. military supplies was rapidly approved to be flown in by military airlift. Significant, too, was a query from the Shaba Task Force to the U.S. Embassies in Brussels and Paris on whether the Belgians or French were going to intervene.[27]

In Brussels, the situation was similar, with the government's crisis cabinet studying the situation. However, the number of Belgians trapped in Kolwezi put the Belgian government under such intense public scrutiny that Washington was spared. By 15 May, although Henri Simonet, the Belgian foreign minister, had already denied that his government was planning to intervene militarily, many members of the Belgian Paracommando Regiment were speculating on whether there would be another Stanleyville. The answer to that question, however, was going to come from Zaire.[28]

In Kinshasa, the French Embassy continued its push for action. By now, Ross had the embassy monitoring the situation on a 24-hour basis. Meanwhile, the GECAMINES headquarters in Lubumbashi had continued its contacts with its personnel inside the rebel-held city. Suddenly, an air of desperation began to cloud reports as the news from Kolwezi grew worse. By 1000, Ross and Gras knew that as of the 14th, the rebels had killed ten Europeans, nine Belgians, and one Italian. The gloom was partially dispersed when Ross received a copy of a message from the Belgian community in Kolwezi to its embassy demanding a Belgian airborne operation. Ross hoped this plea would force the Belgians to react.[29]

In the meantime, Gras had been invited to a cocktail party at the Moroccan ambassador's home to celebrate Morocco's armed forces day. He was not planning to attend until Ross told him to go so he could corner the representative from the Belgian Embassy. With the directness of the French colonel, the order was like setting a bulldog on a kitten: the unfortunate target was Van Sina, the Belgian chargé d'affaires. Gras cornered his victim shortly after Van Sina's arrival, and after the briefest exchange of pleasantries, Gras opened with, "You must know that if you do not decide to intervene, you will be held responsible for the massacres that are going to occur in the coming hours!" When Van Sina replied that such a decision was not his to make, Gras told him that it was his duty to do the impossible and get his government to act rather than dismiss the reports of massacres as exaggerations. Gras concluded his sermon with the admonishment to the astonished Belgian that, "You do not have the right to ignore what is happening!"[30]

As he returned to the embassy, Gras believed that his exhortation should at least have prodded the dispatch of a cable to Brussels demanding an intervention by at least three battalions of Belgian paras. Considering his own situation, Gras concluded that if Paris did decide to act, then the operation was going to take place with little time for planning. To facilitate the operation, Gras decided to create his own little battle staff. Using Larzul to gather as much intelligence information as possible, Gras selected Lieutenant Colonel Philippe Vagner and Commandant Capelli to begin planning for either a combined operation with the Belgians or a French unilateral operation. Vagner was to contact Major Van Melle to begin the planning for the combined operation. At this stage, Gras considered the planning to be a backup measure to the scheme he had put before General Babia to use two French companies to reinforce the 311th and 133d in a drive from the Lualaba bridge. He knew that the two units were already in Lubumbashi, and he assumed they were following his plan. It was the only bad assumption Yves Gras made during the crisis. In doing so, he had failed to consider that Mobutu might take a hand in the situation.[31]

That evening, unknown to Gras, Major Mahele, the commander of the 311th, received a surprising directive to report to President Mobutu's office. An excellent officer in an army with a disastrous record, the thirty-year-old Zairian enjoyed the respect of his French advisers. Although honored, Mahele must have been taken aback when Mobutu ordered him to select a single company to be dropped on Kolwezi the following morning. The remainder of the unit was to push overland from Lubumbashi to link up with the air-dropped unit. President Mobutu, like many politicians, was unable to resist direct involvement in military planning. Colonel Gras' proposed plan served as a basis for the directive; only Mobutu wanted the 311th to carry it out without French troops. A FAZ victory at Kolwezi would restore public confidence in his regime.[32]

The order was absolute madness, but Mahele had little choice but to comply. His unit was only six months old, and only one company, the 1st, had qualified for its wings with a total of six jumps. The 2d had made but four jumps, and the 3d was still in ground school. None of the units had ever made a tactical jump and assembly as part of an operation. Now, Mahele had to select one for an almost guaranteed slaughter. Keeping the 1st Company intact as his most experienced unit and therefore his best bet on reaching Kolwezi quickest, Mahele selected the 2d Company to make the jump. Commanded by Captain Mosala-Monja, a graduate of the U.S. Army Command and General Staff College, the 2d Company, 311th Airborne Battalion, had less than twenty-four hours left in its short life as an effective unit.[33]

V. MASSACRE IN KOLWEZI

At 0630 on 16 May, a single C-130 flying from Lubumbashi opened its jump doors and dropped sixty Zairian paratroops just east of Kolwezi. On the ground, rebel gunners opened fire on the descending troops before they hit the ground. The aircraft had been off its intended course, and many of the troops landed in the surrounding bush. In many respects, they were the fortunate ones; those who landed close to the FAZ headquarters were shot before they could assemble. Only a few made it to the headquarters they were supposed to have saved. At 0900, the same C-130 returned and repeated its earlier performance. The results were equally disastrous. Again, the rebels were able to scatter the inexperienced paras before they could react. Of the 120 members of Captain Mosala-Monja's 2d Company, 311th Airborne Battalion, most were missing, wounded, or dead. In any case, the unit was out of action.[1]

The destruction of the 2d Company, in itself a tragic waste, sparked a greater tragedy in Kolwezi. Colonel Bosangé and around twenty survivors of the 14th Brigade had been holding out against repeated attacks since the invasion began on the 13th. During the morning, the rebels had attacked once already and failed. But the disaster of the 2d Company unnerved the frazzled Zairians. As the next attack began, the Zairian soldiers broke and ran.[2]

As the government troops ran, they left behind around forty Europeans who had taken shelter in the office of Baron-Leveque across the street from the FAZ headquarters. That morning, a Zairian officer had warned them to stay inside until soldiers came to escort them to some helicopters coming from Kinshasa to evacuate them. After the Zairians ran away, the Europeans were surprised to see the Katangans coming up the street. When two Belgian men went outside to talk, the rebels opened fire and killed them. The rebels then turned their weapons on the other Europeans who were crowded into a single room. Two of the expatriates, Gino Jurman and René Michel, managed to escape by using a trap door in the toilet to get up in the ceiling crawl space, where they remained for the next four days. Inside the slaughterhouse, one other survivor struggled to live. Ms. Radu, though bleeding from four wounds, survived, hidden by the thirty-nine bodies of men, women, and children. The massacres had begun in earnest.[3]

In another neighborhood, Maurice Faverjon was in trouble again. This time, the Katangans went to his house and accused him of being a Mirage pilot. Hustling him into the back seat of a Volkswagen, they took Faverjon to their headquarters. Just outside the headquarters,

43

the Katangan driver ran afoul of an officer who had around fifty prisoners kneeling on the sidewalk. Faverjon was convinced that he was about to join the prisoners. However, distracted by his argument with the driver, the officer waved Faverjon away, and he hurried home. Later, Faverjon found out just how lucky he had been when the fifty prisoners were discovered dead in a nearby lake.[4]

While his 2d Company was committed to a suicidal raid, Major Mahele began his overland push to Kolwezi from Lubumbashi, a distance of 150 kilometers via secondary roads. Mahele expected the rebels to defend the route at critical points. He was certain to encounter resistance at the Lualaba bridge, and his strength did not allow for many losses along the way. When Colonel Gras had first proposed an overland drive to the Lualaba bridge, he had based his plan on the idea of using a brigade-size force consisting of the 311th and 133d Battalions and a battalion of military academy cadets. Gras hoped to corset that force with two French paratroop companies. Mahele had far less strength than a brigade. Because of the 2d Company's independent operation, he did not even have a full battalion. Before he could get under way, the FAZ headquarters in Lubumbashi took his 3d Company as a reserve. Instead of a brigade or even a battalion, the 311th began its overland march with 200 of its normal 500-man complement. Mahele had his command section and the 1st Company to begin his drive. By that evening, he was poised on the Lualaba for the final 25-kilometer push to Kolwezi.[5]

Back in Kinshasa, Gras continued working for some sort of intervention. During the morning, he had been on the telephone to Paris repeatedly. Speaking to Colonel Gerin-Roze and General Vanbremeersch of the Military Cabinet at the Élysée and General Loisillon and Colonel Chabert at army headquarters, Gras begged for a French paratroop battalion to use in an airborne operation. He also asked for permission to send the 311th's French advisers to Lubumbashi in order to prepare for the drive on the Lualaba bridge. But Paris had yet to give up on the Belgians taking the lead in an operation in Zaire, even though Foreign Minister Simonet continued to discount the possibility of any intervention.[6]

As d'Estaing's representative in Zaire, André Ross was growing increasingly desperate. The information trickling out of Kolwezi via Lubumbashi steadily worsened, with the number of reported deaths growing larger. Out of frustration, Ross grabbed Gras, and the two visited Mobutu. The audience with the Zairian went strangely. When confronted with the rising death toll, Mobutu dismissed the reports as unconfirmed and proclaimed that the FAZ had the situation "well in hand." Mobutu seemed to have made a drastic recovery from the previous day, when he had asked for all kinds of help. Ross and Gras did not know of the 311th's operation, and Mobutu was waiting for a positive report before telling the world of the FAZ's masterstroke.[7]

Returning to his office, the French ambassador again picked up his pen to try to convince Paris to act. This time, the addressee was President Giscard d'Estaing. Carefully, Ross detailed his concerns: the rebels had 3,000 Europeans as hostages, and they had begun killing them already. Reports had indicated the rebels might attempt to move the hostages to a central location, a move that would make a mass execution possible. The Belgian negotiations were no more than stall tactics and, in any case, had nothing to do with the rebels' actions in Kolwezi. Ross concluded with the dire prediction that unless an airborne operation took place in the next forty-eight hours, a tragedy was going to occur.[8]

Now that Ross had formally joined the advocates for military action, he wanted the intervention to be a combined effort. Ross' ideal operation was a combined French and Belgian airborne operation supported by an American airlift. He had the opportunity to explore these countries' assessments of the situation when a Frenchman from Lubumbashi gave him firsthand information on the deteriorating situation in Kolwezi. Ross then sent the Frenchman to inform the U.S. and Belgian Embassies. The Americans believed the reports and said that they might provide some form of support for a rescue. But the Belgians dismissed the deaths as exaggerations; Brussels was not ready to face the true nature of the situation. Ross' hopes for a combined rescue looked dim.[9]

Gras had already arrived at that conclusion. By now, the Frenchman was like a man possessed. He had been operating on minimal sleep since the crisis began and could feel its effects. Unable to remain inactive, he went to see General Babia to discuss the use of the 311th and 133d Battalions in Lubumbashi. Anticipating a brigade-size drive on Kolwezi, Gras was completely stunned by the revelation that the 2d Company had jumped that morning and the 311th was moving to link up with it at Kolwezi. Though Babia appeared confident, Gras smelled disaster. News of the operation soon spread around the world.[10]

In Washington, D.C., the Shaba Task Force had been disappointed to learn that Morris-Knudsen had postponed the evacuation operation of its Kolwezi base camp. Although the U.S. Embassy had ordered its consulate in Lubumbashi to evacuate quietly all Americans from the danger areas, only Morris-Knudsen had the assets to remove the people from the camp, a measure the local authorities did nothing to support. The FAZ had been rather coy about the idea to begin with, as they hardly wanted to encourage a mass exodus of expatriates from Shaba. Nevertheless, Morris-Knudsen's manager, Mr. Adams, had been ready to order the operation despite veiled warnings from Babia that such an operation was the company's responsibility. But as news came in on the FAZ airborne operation— the Americans at the work camp reported seeing the parachutes— Adams decided to delay the evacuation. Despite assurances from Mobutu that the "Katangans were dispersing in all directions," concern over the expatriates' safety grew as reports of new killings continued to come in via Lubumbashi. Based on the increased threat to the Americans, President Jimmy Carter ordered the 82d Airborne Division to achieve a higher state of readiness. By the following day, the 82d's 2d Brigade was ready to go. The Carter administration made sure that the word was out.[11]

However, the 82d Airborne Division was not the only military unit on alert. Across the Atlantic, the Belgian Paracommando Regiment was also on standby. The elite unit of the Belgian Army, the Paracommandos had a short but proud history. Formed from the Belgian Squadron of the British Special Air Services and the 10th Inter-Allied Commando following World War II, the Paracommando Regiment had seen service in the Belgian Congo and the postindependence Democratic Republic of the Congo. Units of the regiment had intervened in the 1960 upheavals in Leopoldville, and many of the men in the unit had jumped in Operation Dragon Rouge.[12]

Since Dragon Rouge, the regiment had changed somewhat. Rather than just the three battalions of 1964, the unit had added an air-transportable tracked reconnaissance squadron, a 105-mm artillery battery, an antitank company, and a mobilization cell for a fourth battalion. Based on the experience of Stanleyville, the regiment also included a fully air-transportable surgical hospital. Retaining the headquarters for the 1st Para, 2d Commando, and 3d Para Battalions, the regiment had nine independent companies. Based on the Belgian draft system, the regiment rotated its men in fifteen-month cycles. In May 1978, the 3d Para was in its thirteenth month of training, the 1st Para in its sixth month, and the 2d Commando in its third month. Training was the same for all the men. With volunteers manning all the specialized units and noncommissioned officer (NCO) positions, a full 70 percent of the regiment's 2,500 men were professional soldiers.[13]

Equally important to the regiment's reorganization since 1964 was the Belgian Air Force's increased airlift capability. Since the Belgian Air Force possessed a limited number of C-47s and C-54s in 1964, U.S. Air Force C-130s flew the Paracommando Regiment to the Congo. Now, in 1978, the Belgians' 15th Wing, commanded by Colonel Alaine Blume, had ten C-130s and two Boeing 727s, along with the maintenance packages necessary for advanced base operations.[14]

By the evening of the 16th, three of the 15th Wing's C-130 crews were preparing for possible deployment to Zaire. Following the establishment of a crisis cabinet on the 15th, the Belgian government struggled with the Zaire issue for the next twenty-four hours. Though the Zairian Foreign Ministry was in Brussels asking for military hardware, the Belgian government had delayed any response, saying any aid would be constrained by the 2,000 Belgians in the hands of the FNLC. Accordingly, Foreign Minister Simonet directed a full-cabinet review on the 16th, but when the news of the 311th's operation reached Brussels, the review shifted focus to the issue of intervention. Though the Belgians had no intention of a unilateral intervention, Minister of Defense Paul Vanden Boeynants ordered the General Staff to prepare for a discrete evacuation via Kigali, Rwanda. Pulling the plan for Operation Samaritan (a plan completed the previous year during Shaba I) off the shelf, the General Staff ordered the Paracommando Regiment to prepare one company for deployment to Zaire. At 1130 on the 16th, Colonel Henri J. G. ("Rik") Depoorter, commander of the Paracommando Regiment, ordered his 3d Para Battalion to have one company ready by 0300 on the 17th. Concurrently, orders went to the 15th Wing to ready three C-130s to support the plan.[15]

The day was not over yet for Depoorter or Blume. At 1330, the Belgian consul in Lubumbashi had signaled, "Radical change in the attitude of the FNLC toward the Europeans. First victims signaled: first three, then five, the panic is spreading among the expatriates in Kolwezi." The message generated extreme concern in the Belgian government, and at 2300, Depoorter and Blume entered a special meeting at General Staff headquarters. They were to have 1,000 paras ready by 1000 on 18 May for deployment to Zaire.[16]

So ended 16 May 1978. In Kolwezi, the rebels, sparked by the abortive Zairian airborne operation, had turned on their European hostages, and the slaughter was growing by the hour. Outside the city, the 311th was approaching the Lualaba bridge in a futile attempt to save the already destroyed 2d Company. Back in the Zairian capital city, Mobutu bragged on the success of a disastrous military operation, while the Western community realized that intervention was

Mayor General Henri J. G. Depoorter, who commanded the Belgian Paracommando Regiment as a colonel

unavoidable. As the French Embassy attempted to convey to Paris the need for action, the Belgian consul in Lubumbashi had convinced Brussels that a military response was necessary. The Belgian Paracommando Regiment was busily preparing for yet another trip to Africa. At the same time, the U.S. government waited to see whether the majority of the U.S. citizens would be evacuated without employing the 82d Airborne Division.

As dawn broke on 17 May, Major Mahele and his understrength 311th Airborne Battalion continued marching on Kolwezi. Some twenty-five kilometers from Kolwezi, Mahele came upon a company from the 133d Infantry Battalion guarding the bridge. Mahele ordered the unit commander to join his column, thus leaving the crucial bridge unguarded. Moving on westward toward Kolwezi, Mahele ran into an ambush. Despite their greenness, the troops responded well, quickly dismounting and assaulting the ambush. However, the rebels' fire was intense, and Mahele sensed that his men were about to break and run. Mahele sprang forward, rallied his men, and broke the ambush at a cost of four dead and ten wounded troopers.[17]

After reorganizing his troops and caring for the wounded, Mahele moved out once again. Just short of the Kolwezi airport, the 311th struck another ambush. Mahele responded by leading the counterattack, and his men pushed the rebels back. Surging through the scattering rebels, the 311th rallied and drove through to the airport, securing the field by midday. Although the FNLC made a few half-hearted attempts to regain the airfield, Mahele's men held. Luckily, the rebels gave up around dusk, as Mahele's unit was almost out of ammunition. Now, the undermanned unit was almost in as great a danger as the Europeans in Kolwezi.[18]

North of the airfield in the European sectors of the city, the rebels were engaged in "a hunt for whites." William ("Bill") Starkey, an American employee of Morris-Knudsen, had been a virtual prisoner in his home for the past several days. On the 17th, the rebels went to his house and escorted him to the edge of town. After telling him to run, the rebels shot Starkey and left him for dead. Waiting until his assassins had departed, Starkey managed to stumble to the GECAMINES hospital for help. At the lake south of Kolwezi, the fifty prisoners whom Maurice Faverjon had seen the previous day were marched into the water and shot. Other killings took place throughout the city. Many were committed by the locally recruited youth rather than the FNLC regulars. Indiscriminate firing was going on all over the town, including random air attacks by FAZ Mirage fighters. An American Methodist missionary, Harold Amstutz, interrupted a radio contact and pleaded with the authorities to halt the attacks. After seizing and beating the GECAMINES manager for Kolwezi, the rebels forced him to transmit a message that afternoon warning: "Military authorities [invaders] here expect a foreign paratroop intervention. This will be considered an act of war. The situation is very delicate."[19]

Foreign paratroops might have been going to intervene, but by midday, it was clear that they would not be U.S. troops. At 0718, Morris-Knudsen had begun its evacuation of the base camp northwest of Kolwezi. Using helicopters and trucks, the company moved seventy-seven of its people to Musonie. From there, DC-3s flew them to Kananga and safety. By 1512, the evacuation was over. Of the 233 Americans in Shaba, all but 13 were out of danger. As for the unfortunates in Kolwezi, they could only hope that foreign troops would arrive soon.[20] "

On the morning of the 17th, French Ambassador André Ross sat in his office holding another cable from the Belgian consul in Lubumbashi. Intended for Brussels, the cable begged for an intervention within twenty-four hours. Otherwise, warned the Belgian, there would be massacres in Kolwezi. Ross transmitted the

The vital Benguela rail bridge destroyed during the guerrilla war in Angola. The rail line is the main route for Zairian copper shipments to the Atlantic coast.

cable to Paris, praying it would force the Belgian government to act, thus freeing the French authorities from their self-imposed inaction.[21]

But the period of French restraint was ending. At 0700, Colonel Gras received the authority for his Mirage instructor pilots to fly strike missions against the rebels. Heartened by the message, Gras called in the members of his planning team to go over the results of their efforts.[22]

Kolwezi, the focus of the planning effort, was not an easy target. As the center of Zaire's mining industry, Kolwezi produced or processed 75 percent of the copper and 90 percent of the cobalt exported by GECAMINES. The population reflected the importance of the city, consisting of some 143,000 people in a 60-mile radius. Tied to the rest of the country by the Benguela railroad, Kolwezi had grown in a sprawling fashion around the railhead and GECAMINES facilities.[23]

European Kolwezi consisted of two areas referred to as the old town and new town (see map 4). Old town made up the western half of the city and new town the eastern section. The central railroad station linked the two halves, which together covered around eight kilometers east to west and three kilometers north to south. Inside these European districts, the housing was luxurious by African standards, with wide tree-lined avenues, walled-in villas with gardens, and modern facilities such as a hospital, schools, and a cinema.

Outside these districts, Kolwezi was a conglomeration of native towns with crowded company housing for the fortunate or shacks for the majority. The city had two airfields. The main one, some five kilometers south, had an airstrip about four kilometers long. Paved, it could handle C-130s but nothing much larger or heavier. The other strip was the flying club's grass field just north of the old town. Outside the urban areas of Kolwezi was the African bush. Varying from a

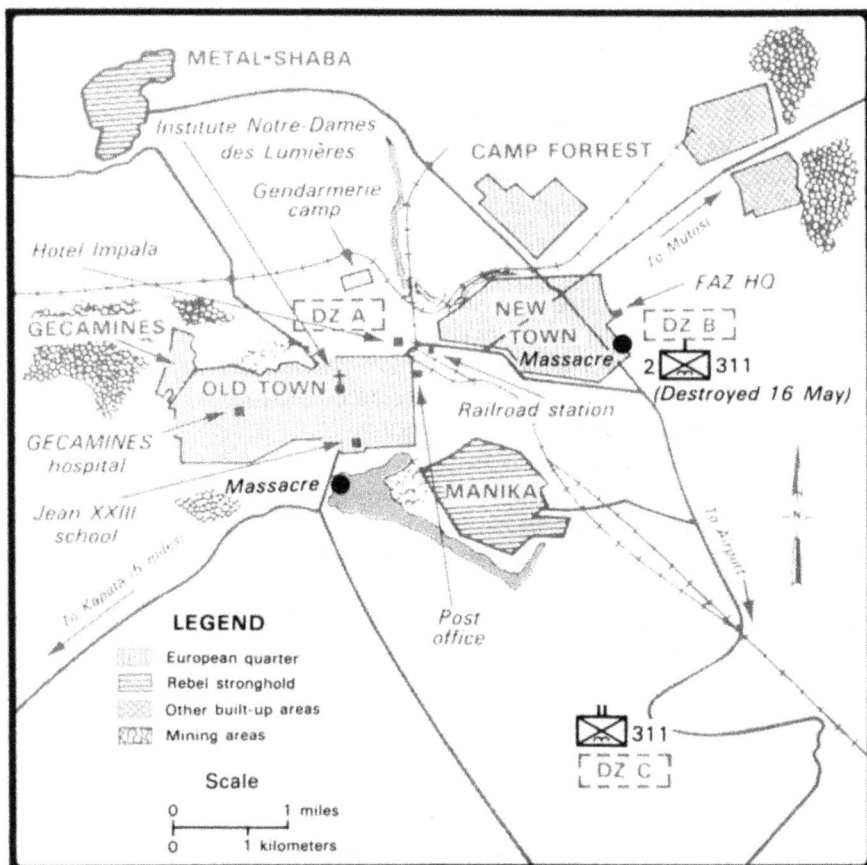

Map 4. Kolwezi, 17 May 1978

dense jungle of towering trees to savanna studded with nine-foot-high termite hills, the bush began at the city's limits. Once outside its confines, eleven-foot-high elephant grass blocked almost all lateral vision, surrounding clearings with miniature forests.

Colonel Gras had given his planners guidance on how he envisioned the operation. Surprise and speed were the critical elements. Only by securing all of the city simultaneously could an attacking force prevent the rebels from turning on the hostages. Such an approach demanded the use of multiple drop zones. But Gras wanted the drop zones on the same east-west axis so that the force commander could shift forces at the last minute without forcing the FAZ pilots to alter their course. He figured the rebels occupied most of the public buildings like the Jean XXIII school, GECAMINES hospital, post offices, and business offices. To reach all these places rapidly required many troops on the ground as soon as possible.[24]

Lieutenant Colonel Vagner accommodated Gras' concept in his study of the problem. He picked two drop zones. First was the old flying club airstrip just north of the old town and west of the new town. Second was the open area east of the FAZ headquarters in the new town. From these two drop zones, the force could fan out into most of the European areas. The plan did involve risk. With the troops jumping beside the city, they would be landing almost on top of the rebels. Gras pointed out that the French had done the same thing successfully in Indochina against a more dangerous foe than the FNLC. By using close air support prior to the operation, the risk of landing on an organized foe could be reduced. Also, there was a danger from shoulder-fired surface-to-air missiles, but Gras accepted the danger as minimal since no missiles had been fired against FAZ Mirages during the week. Less spectacular than the enemy threat but more likely to affect the operation's outcome was the risk of pilot error. If the FAZ pilots were off in their approach, the force might have to land inside the towns or out in the bush. When Vagner suggested using the main airfield, Gras told him to go with the drop zones closer to the city. It would be better to run the risks involved with jumping in close than landing on the airstrip five kilometers from the city. The mission was to rescue the hostages inside the city, not to conduct an airborne operation to seize an airfield. Certainly, the plan entailed risks, and Gras recognized that only a highly trained unit would be able to complete such a mission successfully. Shortly afterward, Gras received a message that removed his doubts about the demand for well-trained and well-led troops. At 1100, Paris notified him that the 2d R.E.P. was on alert for deployment to Zaire.[25]

Five thousand miles away on the island of Corsica, the phone rang in the headquarters of the 2d R.E.P. General Liron, commander of the 2éme Brigade Parachutiste, was calling for Lieutenant Colonel Phillipe Erulin, the 2d R.E.P.'s commander. Taking the phone, Erulin was surprised to hear that he had six hours to prepare his unit for deployment to Zaire. The disbelieving Erulin protested that he would need twenty hours, rather than six, to prepare. Nevertheless, Liron stood by his orders. Erulin ordered the alert signal activated, and Camp Raffali, the unit's home, turned into an ant bed.26

Like the Belgian Paracommando Regiment, the 2d R.E.P. had a short but spectacular career. Created in Morocco in 1948 as the 2éme Batallion Étranger de Parachutistes (2d B.E.P.), the unit deployed to Indochina the following year. From then on, the 2d B.E.P. had fought almost continuously until it was annihilated in the disaster at Dien

The French Foreign Legion in Corsica

Bien Phu. Reconstituted and renamed the 2éme Régiment Étranger de Parachutistes, the unit left Indochina in 1955 after it had lost 775 men. Arriving in Algeria soon afterward, the 2d R.E.P. again found itself fighting in another war, until the French pulled out in 1961. In 1967, the 2d R.E.P. was integrated into the regular French Army as a part of the 11th Airborne Division. Based in Camp Raffali, named after a battalion commander killed in Vietnam, the 2d R.E.P. had continued to respond to calls for overseas duty in places such as Djibouti and Chad.[27]

Though Erulin protested the impossible time schedule, he knew his men could meet it. Two companies of the unit had been on a 48-hour movement status; now, the unit had to upgrade to a six-hour alert with a motorized force, two companies, and a mounted reconnaissance section. The 2d R.E.P had but four line companies, a combat support company, and a headquarters and support company. Each line company specialized in a particular field of combat. The 1st Company was the unit's expert in infantry antitank warfare. The 2d Company concentrated on mountain and winter warfare and the 3d on amphibious techniques, including combat swimmer and scuba skills. The 4th Company practiced the skills of sabotage and sniping. Each unit then taught its particular area of expertise to the remainder of the regiment. The combat support company had a reconnaissance section trained in free-fall parachuting, a mortar section, and a Milan antitank missile section. All told, the 2d R.E.P. had around 700 men. Much like a U.S. Army Ranger battalion, the unit was a formidable foe.[28]

With the present alert, Erulin's major problem was that his regiment was scattered all over Corsica conducting training. He had to recall men from those training areas and get them ready to deploy. Complicating the problem was the unit's chronic shortage of officers. Of the forty-two infantry officers assigned to the 2d R.E.P., ten were deployed elsewhere—seven in Chad—and four had to be used in support capacities that prohibited their deployment. Consequently, Erulin had but twenty-eight officers to conduct the operation. Therefore, he relied heavily on his NCOs to ready the force for movement, and they did not fail him. At 2000, the 2d R.E.P. was ready. When no further word came in, Erulin showed his experience by ordering the troops bedded down. All officers and NCOs received similar instructions as they were released to go home. With a duty officer in each company, the 2d R.E.P. rested and waited.[29]

For Colonel Yves Gras, the waiting was rapidly becoming intolerable. Following the news that the 2d R.E.P. was on alert, Gras and his staff were able to refine their plan to retake Kolwezi. He wished he could count on the support of the Belgian paras to cut off any rebel escape routes, but by this time, Gras had come to discount the cooperation of the Belgians. Instead, he was examining this operation as a French-Zairian effort. When he learned that evening that Major Mahele's 311th Airborne Battalion had pushed on to seize the Kolwezi airfield, Gras was not pleased. He felt the 311th had been overextended and, more seriously, had left the Lualaba bridge unattended. Once again, Gras called the Élysée and demanded action. Asking for the movement of the 2d R.E.P., Gras told General Vanbremeersch that he intended to conduct the operation on the morning of 20 May. At midnight on the 17th, word came back from Paris. The 2d R.E.P. was deploying with four companies and its mortars. Gras was ordered to take command of the operation.[30]

The movement order to the 2d R.E.P. virtually guaranteed the French commitment to intervene. It also sparked a debate between Paris and Brussels over the correct approach to the conflict. In keeping with President d'Estaing's activist approach toward the continent of Africa, France was as much concerned with the reestablishment of Zaire's internal security as in safeguarding the expatriates. The French did not approach the problem as an evacuation operation. The 2d R.E.P., acting under Gras' orders, was going to Zaire to kill rebels in order to save the Europeans. Brussels focused on the expatriates' safety. Despite Belgium's business interests in Zaire and a desire to secure those investments, the government remembered the bitter lesson of the 1964 operation. More expatriates were killed after that intervention than before. Regardless of the alert of the Paracommando Regiment, Brussels still hoped that a negotiated release of the foreigners might take place through the Red Cross. The difference between the two European neighbors was fundamental. Belgium's foreign minister, Simonet, attempted to minimize the dispute by saying, "My French colleague told me that the view of his government was humanitarian but that it also wanted to restore order. It was not a question of any difference in views between Paris and Brussels, but a difference in perspective." Simonet was merely engaged in the diplomatic art of dissimulation.[31]

For the United States, the situation had at the same time become more clear on one hand and more confused on the other. With the success of Morris-Knudsen's evacuation of the majority of the Americans, the pressure on Washington, D.C., to act had diminished dramatically. True, thirteen or fourteen Americans remained in Kolwezi, but the French and Belgians appeared ready—to American

Belgium focused on the expatriates' safety. Here a patrol departs
the GECAMINES mining company.

eyes—to conduct a combined rescue. It did not appear likely that the
82d Airborne Division would be needed. All in all, the crisis so far had
worked to the Carter administration's benefit by allowing it to conduct
a relatively cheap display of determination. All the United States was
going to be required to do was to supply strategic airlift to the French
and the Belgians. That turned out to be more complicated than had
been expected as the possibility of a single combined operation fell
apart. Instead, the United States was going to end up supporting two
independent operations with the same target.[32]

VI. THE WEST REACTS

With the order to assume command of the operation to retake Kolwezi, Colonel Gras slept little the evening of the 17th, nor did Lieutenant Colonel Vagner and Commandant Capelli. Gras had them back at work by 0100. After telling Vagner to plan on using the FAZ airlift, Gras gave his subordinates until 0700 to have the order completed. The FAZ had 5 C-130s, and with 2 additional French C-160s, Vagner could put around 500 rigged paras on the ground in a single lift. A second wave would be needed to get the remainder of the 2d R.E.P. on the drop zone. Vagner and Capelli were up to the task. At 0700, Vagner presented the plan. Approved by Gras, the plan for Operation Leopard was soon on the way to Paris.[1]

At around 0830, a new message came into Gras' office. Gras was amazed to read the latest from Paris; the General Staff wanted to know if Gras could advance the date of the operation from 0630 on 20 May to 19 May. After a quick staff meeting, Gras replied in the negative. He wanted air support, and the FAZ pilots had fired all the ammunition for their Mirage fighters. The resupply of ammunition would have to be flown down from Ndjamena, Chad, and would not arrive until the morning of the 19th. Furthermore, Gras knew that the 2d R.E.P. would need some time to rest and study the plan. To go on the 19th would risk not having enough time to get all the force on the ground before sunset. Therefore, the operation would have to go on the 20th as planned.[2]

Outside factors began to affect the execution of Operation Leopard. During the afternoon, a disgusted André Ross handed Gras a copy of a Radio France International broadcast. Dated that morning, the transcript reported the deployment of 1,100 Belgian Paracommandos and 12 C-130s to Kamina, Zaire. The paras, stated the report, were going to rescue the Europeans in Kolwezi. With the rebels already making threats should the West choose to intervene, both Ross and Gras understood why Paris had asked to move up the date of the operation. As if that were not enough to disturb the rebels in Kolwezi, Gras was stunned to learn that Mobutu had flown his C-130 into the Kolwezi airport. Of course, the Zairian had a full complement of newsmen along to cover the event. With a Mirage conveniently staging a strike in the background, Mobutu met an amazed Major Mahele while the crew off-loaded needed supplies.[3]

While Mobutu made his gesture—a gesture that had caused the loss of the 2d Company of the 311th Airborne Battalion and the lives of over 100 expatriates—the pressure on Gras to act grew steadily. The situation was not without irony as Journiac called Gras at 1500 to repeat the request that the operation take place on the 19th. Telling Gras, "You are the soul judge," Journiac again accepted Gras' negative response. Gras' reasoning for refusing remained the same, plus his chance to coordinate the operation with the Belgians was not completely gone.[4]

At 0700, Gras attended a meeting with FAZ Generals Babia and Ginga, Colonel Geraci of the U.S. Military Assistance Mission in Zaire, Colonel Bleus of the Belgian Military Mission, and Major Van Melle. After Babia had announced Mobutu's safe return, he turned the meeting over to Bleus who gave the arrival schedule for the Paracommando Regiment at Kamina. After sharing the 2d R.E.P.'s schedule, Gras and Bleus agreed on a combined operation. The Belgians were to use eight C-130s from Kamina and the French four FAZ C-130s and four C-160s from Ndjili. The aircraft were to rendezvous over Kamina and attack together. To facilitate planning, the Belgian command group was to fly to Kinshasa for a meeting at 1100 on the 19th. Also, beginning on the 19th, U.S. Air Force C-141s were to ferry in fuel to support the airlift. Babia asked Bleus the Belgians' intentions: "Are you planning an evacuation? That would only take forty-eight hours and would collapse GECAMINES' operation and Zaire's economy." Bleus responded that he thought it was a rescue but promised the troop commander would know. Gras stated that the French were to restore order for the population—both black and white. This meeting was the closest the two NATO allies would come to a combined operation.[5]

Gras left the meeting convinced that Bleus had absolutely no mandate to plan a combined operation with the French. The question became passé when Babia called Gras to his quarters and showed him an intercepted message from the FNLC commander, General Mbumba. The message directed the rebels to kill their hostages, destroy the mines, and evacuate most of the local population. Faced with this increased threat—caused no doubt by news media announcements on the Belgian deployment—and the unlikely possibility of a combined operation with the Belgians, Gras decided to move the date up to the 19th at 0700. When the Zairians promised to have the FAZ C-130s ready, Gras returned to his residence to call General Payrat. Afterwards, Gras held yet another meeting and provided his staff with the new schedule. Vagner was to brief at 0300 on the 19th. At 2200, Gras informed his Zairian, American, and Belgian counterparts of his intentions to act the next day. At 2315,

Lieutenant Colonel Phillipe Erulin, commander of the 2d R.E.P., landed at Ndjili airport.[6]

The movement order had come into the 2d R.E.P.'s headquarters at Camp Raffali at 0220 on 18 May for deployment commencing at 0930. With the Solenarza air base designated as the takeoff site in the order—a good three-hour drive on Corsica's winding roads—Erulin's unit had little time to waste. At 0510, the first truck rolled out the gate, and by 0600, all were on the road. The 2d R.E.P. was deploying in two echelons: the first with 634 men of the assault forces and the second with the 69 drivers for the vehicles that the U.S. Air Force would airlift to Lubumbashi.[7]

The regiment began arriving at Solenarza at 0900. Lieutenant Colonel Alaine Benezit and Captain Stephane Coevoet were to organize the men to board the jets that would fly them to Kinshasa. Supposedly, five DC-8s were to arrive at 0930. Then, the numbers changed to three government-contracted DC-8s, one Air Force DC-8, and one Boeing 707. Since the contracted DC-8s had civilian crews, the troops could not board with weapons. Still, the troops were ready at 0930, and then they waited. At 1130, one aircraft landed with the division commander, General Lacaze, who had come to wish them luck and to tell them that the massacres had already begun in Kolwezi. Finally, the planes arrived, and at 1520, Erulin lifted off in the lead aircraft.[8]

When Erulin boarded his aircraft, he believed that he had until 20 May to get his unit ready to jump on Kolwezi. Now at 2315, 18 May, after a seven-hour flight, he learned that his unit was going into combat the following day. Greeted at the aircraft by Lieutenant Colonels Vagner and Ballade, Erulin took the change in stride. Less than fifteen minutes later, he had Benezit and Capelli figuring manifests for five C-130s and two C-160s. Meanwhile, Erulin and Vagner studied the plan. Again, time was limited; the briefing was to be at 0300, and the first wave was to go at 0700.[9]

The appointed briefing hour, 0300, came and went as a frustrated Vagner waited for a missing Colonel Gras. All of the 2d R.E.P.'s command group had been on the ground since 0200, and they were anxious to get on with the briefing. By this time, it was clear that the last two aircraft would not arrive until 0830, and the initial wave of four companies would have to be reduced. With his prospective audience clearly showing signs of frustration, Vagner began the briefing around 0330.[10]

Bommier, a retired French officer and former attaché in Kinshasa, presented a summary of the problems leading up to the crisis. Now working as a logistics adviser to the FAZ, Bommier knew the subject well, and he proceeded to delve into Zairian history since 1960. Gradually, he covered the evolution of the FNLC and its turbulent past. Vagner knew the long-winded Bommier was in trouble when he heard one wag in the audience mutter, "Before he finishes the war will be over."[11]

Just as the tedious speaker finished, an agitated Gras walked into the room and began the operation briefing. Of all the mornings to have a flat tire, Gras' luck had dictated this one—with the added touch of a missing jack. Actually, the French colonel was lucky to be alive after blowing a tire at 120 kilometers per hour. His luck improved, however, and he had managed to wave down a passing Belgian to get to the airport. Determined to portray an air of confidence, he walked into the briefing and began without bothering to wash the dirt from his hands.[12]

Gras gave a summary of his concept for taking the city. The 2d R.E.P. would first take the old and new towns to secure the European areas, then the airport should an air evacuation become necessary. To accomplish these tasks, Gras said an initial assault of a small headquarters element, two companies, and the mortars—some 405 men—would drop on the flying club strip. This assault would seize likely rebel positions throughout the two towns. If possible that same day, a second wave of 2 more companies of 200 men was to jump either on the flying strip or on drop zone B east of the new town. Once the town was completely secured, the 2d R.E.P. would link up with the FAZ at the main airfield. With that, he turned the briefing over to Vagner.[13]

Reviewing the enemy situation, Vagner began his presentation. The enemy was believed to control most of Kolwezi with several thousand well-armed men. Though it had been reported that the enemy had begun a westerly withdrawal on the 18th, it was certain that 1,000 to 2,000 rebels remained in the area of Kolwezi. These rebels had heavy weapons and might have French AML armored cars taken from the FAZ. Also, the FNLC had probably established strongpoints in the Hotel Impala, the GECAMINES hospital, and the post office in the old town. In the new town, the rebels probably controlled the railroad bridge that linked the two European quarters along with the principal municipal centers like the market and gas station. Vagner pointed out that Manika was the rebels' base of support and would be the most difficult area to control. He also warned the men that the enemy would be able to fire at them as they exited their aircraft. But he concluded that the rebels would probably not mount a concerted counterattack. More likely, the rebels would react with uncoordinated actions before withdrawing.[14]

As for the friendly situation, Vagner reported that more than 2,000 Europeans were under rebel control in Kolwezi. He warned that some had already been killed and others were hostages in locations such as the Jean XXIII school or GECAMINES hospital. Concerning the FAZ, it controlled the main airfield but nothing else. According to Vagner, the local population could be considered neutral, except for those living in Manika.[15]

Giving the mission, Vagner briefed that the 2d R.E.P. would parachute on 19 May on Kolwezi to regain control of the city as rapidly as possible, reestablish and maintain order, and protect the expatriates (see map 5). To accomplish this, the regiment would jump in two waves: the first with three companies on drop zone A and the second with two companies on either drop zones A or B, depending on how the situation developed. Ending the formal briefing at 0430, Vagner worked with Erulin to assign company missions under the concept of the operation.[16]

The 1st Company, jumping on drop zone A, was to move as rapidly as possible into the southern part of the old town to take the Jean XXIII school. The company was to cut off rebel movement to the south and clean out the area between the school and the Institute Notre-Dames des Lumières all the way to the southern edge of the town. Also jumping on drop zone A was the 2d Company, which was to assemble along the west side of the drop zone. Moving alongside the west of 1st Company, the 2d Company was to take the GECAMINES hospital, liberate any hostages found there, and cut off rebel movement to the west. Special instructions to the 2d Company included searching the GECAMINES garages for vehicles suitable for use by the regiment. The 3d Company was to jump on drop zone A in the first wave and to move east and south, taking the bridge between the two towns and the Hotel Impala and the post office. It was to cut off all movement between the two towns and the native quarter of Manika. The 3d Company had as its area of responsibility all of the old town east of 1st Company's zone and was to be prepared for operations into the new town.[17]

The second wave was to be the 4th Company, the scout platoon, and the mortar platoon. The 4th was to jump on either drop zone, depending on the situation. If it jumped on A, the 4th would go into the

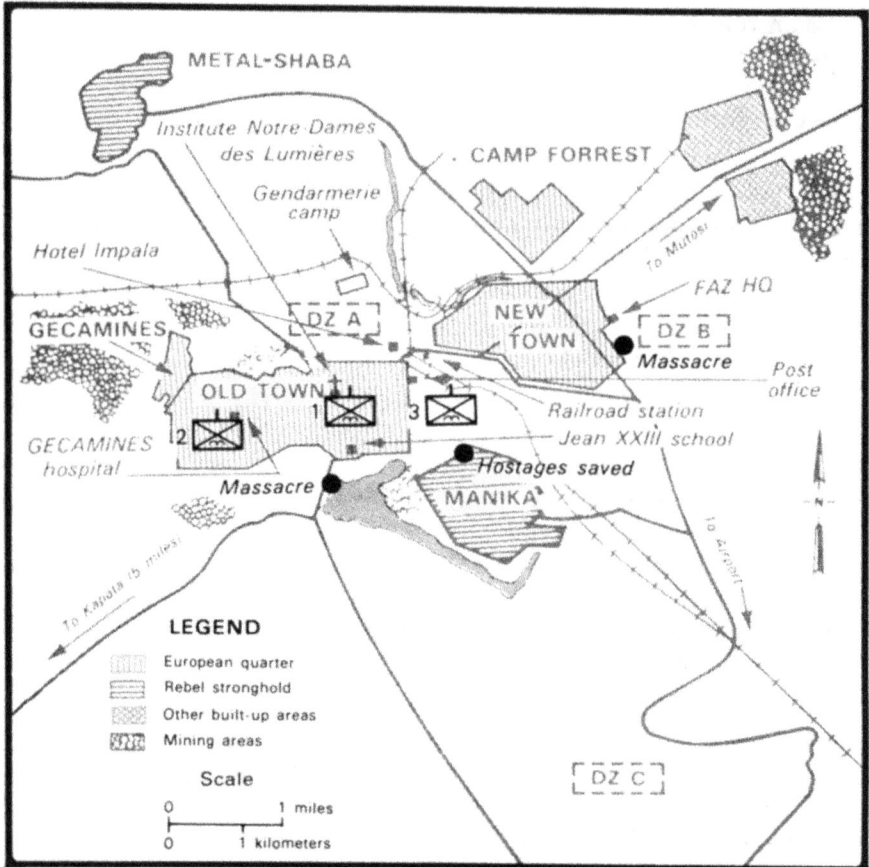

Map 5. Kolwezi, 19 May 1978

old town; if it used drop zone B, the 4th was to take the new town from the rear. The scouts were to jump on drop zone A and clean out the old gendarmerie camp along with Camp Forrest. As for the mortar platoon, it was to establish a firing position just off drop zone A to support the regiment.[18]

The 2d R.E.P. also received special instructions. The men were not to fire unless fired on. Rather than attempt to pull out the expatriates, the men were to encourage the foreign population to remain in place. Should a movement of the Europeans become necessary, central collection points were to be established as needed. Using these rules of engagement and the scheme of maneuver developed by Vagner, Erulin told his company commanders that they were to occupy critical crossroads and junctions inside the towns. Establishing ambushes and checkpoints at these designated points, the regiment would be able to halt all movement after dark. Consequently, the rebels would not be able to escape with any hostages. After the jump, the units were to move as quickly as possible to these positions without stopping to collect their wounded. Though indiscriminate fire was prohibited, Erulin told his men to make every shot fired a kill. He wanted his men to force the rebels "to abandon the hostages in order to save their own skins."[19]

It was an audacious plan, and as such, it held risks. First, it put a great deal of trust in the FAZ C-130 pilots to put the men on the drop zone. Vagner and Gras recognized this risk, and both hoped the pilots were better than the Zairians who flew for "Air Peut-être [air perhaps]," as Air Zaire was commonly called. Furthermore, the operation would be going without the hoped-for close air support, since there was insufficient time to get the Mirage ammunition in from Chad. The other major risk was the need to get both waves in before dark. Otherwise, the Europeans in the new town would be at the rebels' mercy overnight. Time was essential, and delays began to gnaw at the operation.[20]

Part of the second wave of French paratroops on drop zone A on 20 May

64

Gradually, enough of the 2d R.E.P. arrived in Kinshasa to make up the first wave. Thanks to France maintaining semipermanent overflight clearance in most of Africa, the airlift was to take a direct route. Still, the diversion of two aircraft to Abidjan, the Ivory Coast, had forced the first wave to be reduced to three companies. In addition, there were other problems. The French had borrowed parachutes from the FAZ, and these parachutes, American T-10s, would not accept the snap hooks on the French equipment bags. Many of the Legionnaires had to wire the bags to their harnesses. Nevertheless, the 2d R.E.P. was loaded and ready by 0700, but a heavy fog set in and added further delays. Just when the weather began to clear, Gras' duty officer from the embassy appeared and told him the jump was canceled. Apparently, Paris had changed its mimd.[21]

Convinced by Erulin to try to reverse the decision, Gras raced back to the embassy. Calling the Élysée, Gras reached Journiac, who informed him that the operation had not been canceled and to get on with it. After confirming the new order with army headquarters, Gras radioed the airfield and ordered Erulin to take off. The men of the 2d R.E.P. scrambled to rerig and reboard their aircraft. The French had to

French paratroops had difficulty adjusting the American T-10 parachutes
to their French leg bags. Many Legionnaires wired the bags to their harnesses

look for the FAZ pilots who had promptly wandered off when the cancellation order had arrived. Just as they were nearly ready, one C-130 failed. Benezit and Coeveot pulled the men off that aircraft and divided them among the other planes. Then, a C-160 Transall went down, and they had to repeat the performance. By now, every aircraft had eighty to eighty-five rigged Legionnaires on board rather than the specified limit of sixty-four. To climax the circus of confusion, another C-160 had a flat tire, which required another agonizing hour to repair. Finally at 1040, the four C-130s and single C-160 began to take off. By 1104, all were airborne, followed by Gras in the other C-160 as a flying command post.[22]

For the rigged jumpers, the next five hours were pure agony. Normally a four-hour flight, it took five as the lead C-130 got lost. Fortunately, Gras' pilot detected the error in time to get the planes back on course. Still, it was another delay added to the operation. Inside the aircraft, the Legionnaires alternately were chilled from the air conditioning or sweltered with it turned off. As the flight approached Kolwezi at around 1500, it was absolutely impossible to shift the men enough to raise the seats for a jump run. At 1512, the red warning light went on, and the prejump sequence of commands began. The troops were unable to safety check each other; they could only wait in agony until jumping out the door. On one aircraft, Chief Sergeant Paul Fanshaw, an American, struggled in vain to get his stick of jumpers in the correct order. Fanshaw, 2d Section sergeant of the 3d Company, knew his men were tired; they were now into their third day with little sleep. Now, they were going to jump from an unfamiliar aircraft using American parachutes. At 1515, the jump doors went up, and the drop zone flashed by 600 feet below. After an initial dry run to verify the drop zone, the flight swung around for another try.[23]

After yet another fruitless pass, the jump began at 1540—under trying conditions. The FAZ pilots failed to slow down and did not maintain proper altitudes relative to the other aircraft. One C-130 narrowly missed a stick of jumpers by breaking hard to the right of the drop zone. Wind speed was high, with an equally high rate of descent due to Kolwezi's 1,500-meter altitude above sea level; the Legionnaires were moving laterally as fast as they were vertically. Even using the large American chutes, the Legionnaires slammed into the ground. One unfortunate Legionnaire, Strata, was towed; his static line had failed to release his chute. An experienced parachutist, Strata came down on his reserve chute after his jumpmaster cut him free. Unfortunately, the high winds were out of the north and were pushing the men into the old town. Soldiers landed in gardens, on houses, or in trees. Some, like Erulin, landed on top of termite hills, only to fall another nine feet to the ground. Many were simply lost in the elephant grass. One entire antitank section was missing for the next twenty-four hours. The rebels fired at the Legionnaires, but most of the firing was ineffective. Nonetheless, the 2d R.E.P. had already suffered its first dead. Corporal Arnold, 3d Section, 1st Company, was found dead two days later, still in his harness. Still, the unit assembled within ten minutes.[24]

The 3d Company soon found itself in a spirited fight. After vainly searching for his radioman, Captain Gausseres, the commander, linked up with his 2d Section under Lieutenant Wilhelm. Using the section's radio, Gausseres confirmed that his company was assembled and then ordered it to move. Lieutenant Bourgain, the 1st Section's leader, had already had a taste of what lay ahead. Landing in the garden of the Hotel Impala, Bourgain found himself staring at twenty-four pairs of hands—white hands that had been neatly severed at the wrists. Since the hotel was his initial objective, Bourgain gathered his men and charged the building. Inside the hotel, it was worse than in the garden; the shaken officer found twenty bodies. When Bourgain radioed in the information, Erulin came on the net and asked if the casualties were white or black. When Bourgain replied that they were all black, Erulin told him to search the hotel for the six missing French advisers. In complying, Bourgain failed to find the Frenchmen, but he did find what appeared to be their logbook.[25]

Meanwhile, Wilhelm and Fanshaw had reached the overpass connecting the two towns. As Fanshaw set up his defense, he counted heads and came up six short. With only two machine guns and a grenadier, Fanshaw needed heavier weapons. He sent a man to look for the section's weapons container. Just as Corporal Moran returned with the section's rocket launcher, three Panhard AML armored cars came roaring out of the new town. One, an AML 60, charged the section's position, and Moran let it close to thirty meters before knocking it out. A second armored car, a heavier AML 90, also fired on the section only to be destroyed by a rifle grenade. The third withdrew shortly afterward.[26]

While Fanshaw battled the armored cars, the rest of the 3d Company moved to cut the principal route out of Manika into the old town. Adjutant Ivanov and the 3d Section got into a long-range duel with snipers firing from the roof of the Notre-Dames Church. His section and the 3d Company's command group were pinned down, but Bourgain's snipers, using French F-1 sniper rifles with four-power telescopic sights, engaged the rebels and killed three. The 3d Company resumed its movement toward the entrance to Manika.[27]

As Bourgain's section approached the bridge, the rebel fire intensified. He sent a squad to maneuver against the bridge, supported by a barrage of rifle grenades to force the rebels back. Threatening their left flank with his third squad, Bourgain took the bridge, cutting off rebel infiltration from Manika. On his southern flank, his snipers, under the direction of Sergeant Touami, had killed 10 rebels with head shots at ranges in excess of 300 meters. The rebels were concentrated around the École Technique Officiale, and Bourgain ordered his section NCO, Sergeant Moreau, to take the building. While Corporal Callerf enfiladed the rebel withdrawal route with his machine gun, Moreau took the school. Callerf stopped the rebels from retreating six times, each time killing one of the FNLC. When Bourgain got to the school, he found that the rebels had left nine dead behind, along with their weapons.[28]

By this time, Bourgain realized that he was in an overextended position. Just as he started to order his men back to safer positions, one Legionnaire heard French voices coming from the nearby police camp. Upon being told of the French cries, Bourgain yelled out, "Armée Francaise!" and received an immediate response from the refugees. Realizing the people were hostages in a building filled with rebels, Bourgain assaulted the position. Just as the lieutenant kicked the door of the building open, he spotted and killed a rebel who held an armed grenade. In the act of throwing the grenade into a room with twenty-six Europeans and nine blacks, the rebel collapsed and let the explosive roll back toward Bourgain. Reacting quickly, the lieutenant dived back out the door as the grenade exploded harmlessly in the entrance of the building.[29]

Bourgain's actions turned out to be the only incident where direct military action saved hostages from being killed. The reports of a rebel withdrawal were true—as were the reports of massacres in the city. But for the most part, the killings had reached their peak on 16 and 17 May. Most of the FNLC regulars departed for Angola on the 18th. However, the rebels' locally recruited militia and some regulars had remained behind. These were the forces fighting the 2d R.E.P.[30]

In any case, the thirty-five people huddled in the old gendarmerie barracks were certainly happy to see Lieutenant Bourgain. One, Charles Dornacker, had been arrested the 16th along with many of his companions. During the hostages' stay in the camp, the rebels had threatened them with "trial" almost every day, and they had also

French snipers like this one proved to be extremely effective in the Shaba II operation

witnessed daily executions, principally among the natives. As the 2d R.E.P. jumped that afternoon, a mob had attacked the captives' cell, trying to drag them outside to slaughter. By tying their shirts together into a rope, Dornacker and another European, Frédéric Hautot, had managed to tie the cell door closed against the best efforts of the mob who, fortunately for the prisoners, were only armed with clubs. When the prisoners first heard the firing outside, they wisely waited to cry out until they could identify voices. After Bourgain had killed their would-be murderer, the captives swarmed over the surprised and embarrassed French officer. Many began singing the "Marseillaise," the French national anthem. A number of the refugees were wounded, including women and children. One little 2½-year-old girl had been shot. Another was covered in her mother's blood; her wounds were intangible but real. Bourgain had his men gather the shaken survivors and escort them back to the nearby school for the evening. With Bourgain's seizure of the camp, the 3d Company had secured its initial objectives.[31]

During the 3d Company's fight for its objectives, the rest of the 2d R.E.P was engaged in securing the remainder of the old town. The 1st Company commander, Captain Michel Poulet, had assembled his unit for its drive to take the Jean XXIII school. Placing his three sections on parallel streets headed south toward the school, the company commander moved out. As the Legionnaires eased cautiously along the streets, the expatriate population began to come out of hiding. The 1st Section, under Lieutenant Rochon, took the school and discovered ten refugees hiding in the basement. Meanwhile, one expatriate had offered to guide Poulet to a rebel command post. Sending the 2d and 3d Sections to invest and take the Institute Notre-Dames des Lumières convent, Poulet and his command section moved with their guide to the suspected rebel position. His 2d Section reported light contact with the rebels near the convent, who fled after sustaining several losses. Then, Poulet's group moved unhindered toward its objective. After securing the rebel position in a short fight, Poulet discovered several enemy documents that turned out to be the operations orders for the FNLC plan to seize Shaba. Moving out to the company's objective—the isthmus of land between the two small lakes on the town's southern limit—Poulet soon found himself walking through a slaughterhouse; the streets were lined with bodies, both black and white. Finally reaching the objective, Poulet discovered the massacre site at the lake's edges. The 1st Company had secured its objectives.[32]

Just west of the 1st Company's area of operations, the 2d Company was moving to secure the GECAMINES hospital. Under the command of Captain Dubos—known as "Bobosse" to his men—the unit was also to secure the hospital, the western grounds of the Institute Notre-Dames des Lumières, and the GECAMINES garages (to look for vehicles). Despite repeated contacts with rebel forces along the route, Dubos' men moved well under fire, responding as if it were a drill. By dark, Dubos had the hospital, which was almost totally destroyed and proved to be useless, and his other objectives. The 2d Company's seizure of the hospital meant that the first wave of the 2d R.E.P. had completed all its initial missions before sunset. As the night closed on Kolwezi, Erulin could hear his second wave circling above the city.[33]

For the second wave of Operation Leopard, 19 May had been a series of frustrations. Shortly after the initial wave had taken off for Kolwezi, the second had boarded an Air Zaire DC-10 for Kamina. With Kamina less than an hour's flying time from Kolwezi, Colonel Gras hoped to make up for lost time by having the second wave close at hand. On board the DC-10, the 4th Company, the scouts, and the mortar section attempted to get some needed sleep on the way to Kamina. Along with the remainder of the 2d R.E.P.'s headquarters element, the DC-10 also carried Colonel Larzul, Lieutenant Colonel Vagner, Commandant Capelli, and the 311th Airborne Battalion's advisers under Lieutenant Colonel Ballade. All hoped to join in the action to retake Kolwezi. At 1600, the DC-10 landed at Kamina, and its passengers stirred expectantly. Minutes passed, and on asking, the French learned that Kamina did not have a ladder high enough to service a DC-10. A minor frustration became a serious problem as the Legionnaires sat and waited—losing precious time. Finally, a Belgian worker at the field came to their rescue with an ordinary painter's ladder placed on top of an embarkation ramp.[34]

Even hurrying as rapidly as possible, the 250 men of the second wave still had to draw parachutes and rig for the operation. That required time, and it was 1800 before the C-130s could take off for Kolwezi. Forty minutes later, the aircraft swung in on the jump run, waiting for a signal as to which drop zone the paras were to use. Circling over the city, the pilots received the abort signal from Gras in his flying command post. After conferring with Erulin, Gras decided to postpone the second wave. On the ground, Erulin had the old town secured, the western portion of the new town under control, and the entrance to Manika sealed off. Night had already fallen, but the moon had yet to appear. Putting the second wave out in the intense darkness only risked confusion and a strong possibility of the men firing on each other. Although he was not pleased, Gras made the correct decision. After making a futile pass over the airfield to raise the 311th Airborne on the radio, Gras turned for Kinshasa.[35]

As the evening closed in on Kolwezi, Erulin studied the results of the operation so far with Captain Thomas, the intelligence officer of the 2d R.E.P. Since the beginning of the airborne operation at 1540, the regiment had liberated at least 35 hostages, killed around 100 rebels, destroyed 2 AML armored cars, and captured several hundred small arms. In addition, the regiment had captured documents that established the FNLC's strength and purpose in this second invasion, proving Gras' suspicions that this was indeed an attempt to wrest all of Shaba from Zaire. Unaware of Legionnaire Arnold's death, Erulin placed friendly casualties at three to four wounded, five missing, and six jump injuries. The 2d R.E.P. controlled the old town, part of the new town, and the entrance into Manika. For the rest of the evening, Erulin ordered his companies to set up ambushes, taking advantage of the full moon. For the Legionnaires, these nighttime activities were just part of their duties and included their third day without sleep.[36]

With his command post in the Jean XXIII school, Erulin monitored the night's operations. Once again, the 3d Company seemed to be the most aggressive of his units. Adjutant Ivanov of the 3d Section reported early in the evening that his men had found two European families hiding in their sector. The terrified—and starved— expatriates had been hidden since the morning of the 13th. Next, based on the debriefing of Charles Dornacker, Erulin ordered Captain Gausseres to send a patrol into the new town to search for a suspected slaughterhouse near the former FAZ headquarters.[37]

Gausseres decided to go himself, taking a small but well-armed escort. Setting out, the patrol had only gone a few hundred meters when Gausseres began to smell the stench of rotting bodies. Soon, the horrified Frenchman could see bodies scattered around the street, eaten and being eaten by dogs. Gausseres attempted to drive off the dogs and, failing at that, considered opening fire on them. Suddenly, firing broke out back in the 3d Company's sector, and Lieutenant Wilhelm reported that several rebels had attempted to run a roadblock in a Volkswagen. The lieutenant's men had opened fire, killing one and driving the others off. Hearing the report and asking Gausseres how his search was proceeding, Erulin decided the mission could wait until first light. He ordered Gausseres to return.[38]

As the captain turned back, one of his unit's listening posts warned him that six rebels were headed toward his position. Gausseres and his men established a hasty ambush and waited. After what seemed ages, the Legionnaires spotted the rebels and opened fire, killing four and recovering five weapons. Aside from a brief firefight near dawn between the 2d Company and a group of rebels, the remainder of the night was fairly quiet, broken only by occasional firing and the incessant growling of the feasting dogs. The 2d R.E.P welcomed the morning's light.[39]

VII. THE EVACUATION OF KISANGANI: "STANLEYVILLE II"

Forty minutes flying time to the north of Kolwezi, other European soldiers eagerly waited for dawn on 20 May. They were the men of the Belgian Paracommando Regiment, and they, too, had a mission to perform in the mining center.

Following his meeting with the Belgian crisis cabinet the evening of the 16th, Colonel Rik Depoorter, the regiment commander, had returned to his headquarters to begin planning. Actually, the staff was already ahead of the cabinet in anticipating a larger operation than that conceived under Operation Samaritan. At 0200 on 17 May, the Belgian General Staff confirmed the planning guidance: Depoorter was to plan for a seizure of Kolwezi airport and a humanitarian evacuation operation not to exceed seventy-two hours. Based on an enemy strength of around 4,000 rebels, the staff began planning on how best to seize the mining center. Although efforts were still ongoing to secure French cooperation, Depoorter's instructions did not mention the possibility of French assistance. While he went to yet another cabinet meeting that morning, the regimental staff continued its preparations, and by 1500, the plan for Operation Red Bean was ready.[1]

Red Bean called for two reinforced battalions of the regiment to conduct simultaneous airborne operations to seize the airfield and the city the morning of the 20th. The 3d Para Battalion, commanded by Major BEM G. Couwenberg, was to take the flying club airstrip north of the city and move immediately to secure the expatriates. Couwenberg understood the need for speed, for he had written a paper on the Dragon operations while a student at the Belgian Staff College. Along with its headquarters company, the battalion was to have three rifle companies: the 15th and 17th from the 3d Para and the 14th from the 2d Commando Battalion. Meanwhile, the 1st Para Battalion, under the command of Lieutenant Colonel R. Verbeke, was to jump on the main airstrip south of the city. The 1st Para, a veteran of Dragon Rouge, was to take its headquarters company and the 11th, 13th, and 21st Companies. Using 18 radio jeeps, 10 armored jeeps from the reconnaissance squadron, and 26 three-wheeled AS-24s, the regiment was to have 1,180 men for the operation. In addition to its normal medical complement, the regiment was also taking an airborne-qualified surgical team. The regiment would also receive a light aviation detachment with an Alouette helicopter to facilitate control. To move the Paracommandos, the 15th Wing was going to use 10

C-130s and 10 Boeing 727s (8 from Sabena), and the U.S. Air Force was to fly 120 tons of fuel per day into Kamina. While seven of the C-130s were available immediately, three would have to join the airlift at Kamina from a food relief mission in Mali.[2]

Clearly, the Belgian Paracommandos approached the rescue operation as a serious military undertaking. Many of the plan's fundamentals were directly related to the unit's experiences in 1964. Of particular importance to the planners was that the regiment have sufficient strength to take the town and the airstrip at the same time. In executing Dragon Rouge, the Paracommandos had been delayed in seizing the city of Stanleyville (Kisangani), and the Simba rebels had slaughtered many of their hostages moments before the Belgians could save them. The need for trauma medical care was equally important to the operation, which had also been proved in the 1964 operations—hence, the inclusion of the mobile surgical hospital. Finally, the regiment was taking its organic transport to allow it to operate outside the city in motorized patrols as it had done in Dragon Noir, the rescue at Paulis (Isira) in 1964.[3]

Aside from the military lessons learned from 1964, it was equally apparent that Belgium's political leaders had also learned a fundamental lesson. This became apparent in Defense Minister Paul Vanden Boeynants' guidance to Depoorter as the regimental commander departed at 1900 with the tentative decision to execute Red Bean: Depoorter was to execute a humanitarian evacuation operation, taking all measures to protect the expatriates and rescuing any hostages short of crossing international borders. The defense minister prohibited Depoorter from participating in the French operation in any way, classifying it as a military action divorced from the Belgian evacuation. In addition, Depoorter's orders emphasized speed of execution: he had but seventy-two hours to evacuate all refugees who wished to leave. The Belgian government did not intend to abandon any expatriates in Kolwezi as it had done in the hasty withdrawal from the Congo in 1964, nor did it intend to get drawn into a security operation with the French that might backfire on Belgians in other locations in Zaire. So, as Depoorter departed for his headquarters, he understood clearly the political constraints and imperatives surrounding his mission.[4]

With the conditional order to proceed in his pocket, Depoorter put out the formal alert order at 2020 on 17 May for a 1300 departure the following day. The Paracommando Regiment readied for deployment. Major André Patte, a veteran of Dragon Rouge as well as Depoorter's intelligence officer, had managed to develop more information on the situation courtesy of Mr. Lauwers, a GECAMINES employee specially flown in from Zaire. Even with Lauwers' help, Patte still lacked sufficient maps to equip the regiment. By this time, most of the units involved were already preparing to move. Since the decision to execute was not firm, the men of the regiment were not confined to their camps but were released to go home as soon as their preparations were completed.[5]

At 1000 the next day, Depoorter and his staff met with the representatives of Sabena Airlines and the 15th Wing. The officers agreed that the C-130s would deploy first with equipment and parachutes to Kamina. The military and Sabena jets would then move the regiment's personnel. By doing so, the men would remain fresh and rested for the operation on the 20th. To the Paracommandos' chagrin, however, Sabena insisted on using the international airport at Melsbroek rather than Kleine-Brogel. The civilian airlines furthered confusion by continuously changing the number of aircraft available. Overflight clearances were also a problem; unlike France, Belgium had to negotiate clearances with the countries along the route—Morocco, the Ivory Coast, Gabon, and Zaire (Madeira, Abidjan, Libreville, and Kamina). By C-130, the trip would take twenty-five hours, by 727, eighteen hours, but it was the most direct route open to the Belgians.[6]

Even as the men worked, the government announced the alert to the public—to the great consternation of the Paracommandos. As the unit moved to the airport, the regiment was swamped by civilians. The scene at Melsbroek was, according to one of the paras, something out of a circus. News media coverage of the deployment had attracted a large crowd at the airport to watch the regiment take off. Families came out to wave farewell, and the troops lined up for a hurried series of vaccinations. Each 727 was packed with 180 paras along with their rucksacks and weapons. Even with all the delays, the unit was soon loaded, though it was a far cry from the quiet deployment of 1964. That afternoon, the Paracommando Regiment began another journey to Zaire.[7]

At 1315, the first C-130 lifted off with Colonel Blume at the controls. On board were Depoorter and his principal staff. The Belgians were going without air clearance from the French, and it was not until the third C-130 took off that France granted overflight clearance to the Belgians. Nevertheless, it was a remarkable performance by the paras and the flight crews, for less than thirty hours from the initial warning order, the regiment's lead elements were airborne and headed for Africa. That evening, the remainder of the unit, on board the 727s, followed.[8]

After a long and tiresome flight, the first Belgian 727 landed at Kamina at 1400 on 19 May. Greeted by Commandant De Keyser of the regiment's advance party, the paras were off-loading as Depoorter's C-130 set down. The regiment's planes arrived singly at the airfield until, less than thirty-six hours after its departure, the Paracommando Regiment had arrived fully equipped in Zaire.[9]

On landing, Depoorter wasted little time. While the men off-loaded equipment and prepared for the next day's operation, the regimental commander studied the situation in light of a dramatically altered situation. Depoorter had known that the 311th Airborne Battalion reportedly held the Kolwezi airport, but since departing Belgium, he had not received any information on the status of the city or the expatriates. He and his staff, however, were absolutely astounded to learn that the French were to attempt to take the town that afternoon using four to six aircraft. Depoorter feared the French would be unable to secure the city before dark, thus leaving part, if not all, of the expatriates at the rebels' mercy. After learning of the French plan, Depoorter radioed Brussels and asked for permission to conduct a reconnaissance in force into the airfield before dark to reinforce the 2d R.E.P. Although Brussels' reply to the hasty operation was negative, the government did issue the final clearance for the operation on the 20th.[10]

With Brussels' final decision in hand, Depoorter modified his plan to meet the new circumstances in Kolwezi. Since the 311th held the airfield and the French would already be in the town, Depoorter decided to abandon the original plan to parachute onto the two drop zones. Instead, he would conduct an assault landing using the C-130s of Blume's 15th Wing. The two commanders had worked together many times perfecting the technique, and they soon had a workable plan.[11]

At 2200, Depoorter briefed the new plan for Operation Red Bean. Using eight C-130s, the Paracommando Regiment would conduct an air assault landing on Kolwezi airfield in three waves. The first wave was to consist of the regimental tactical command post and elements of the 1st and 3d Para Battalions. The 1st Para Battalion was to secure the airfield while the 3d Para Battalion moved along the railroad into the old town. As soon as the first wave was out of the C-130s, the aircraft would return to Kamina for the next wave. Along with the remainder of the 1st and 3d Para Battalions, the second wave was to bring in the reconnaissance squadron as the regimental reserve. This would free the 1st Para Battalion to move on the new town. The third wave of the assault was to bring in the regiment's vehicles and the mobile surgical hospital. Immediately on arrival at the airfield, the regiment was to set up a reception center for the refugees.[12]

Depoorter's plan capitalized on the new circumstances of the situation. By conducting an air assault on the airfield, he could have 500 paras on the ground and assembled in minutes. Thus, the march into the city could be made in almost the same amount of time as that needed to assemble after an ordinary airborne operation. Without more details on the French operation, Depoorter did not dare drop his men on a drop zone closer to the city—and his orders forbade direct coordination with the French should he be able to contact them. With his full complement of vehicles due in by the third wave, Depoorter could expect to be fully mobile by midmorning. This would allow the regiment to mount patrols outside the city, a capacity sorely missed by the 2d R.E.P. After preparing for the mission, the Paracommando Regiment bedded down for a short night. The men were confident and, in the words of Captain Wittemans, "very calm. Some of them had been at Stanleyville and Paulis. They served as a model for the others." Wittemans spoke from experience: he, too, was a veteran of Dragon Rouge.[13]

The veterans of the airborne assault on the 19th were equally calm. As dawn broke on the 20th, the members of the 2d R.E.P. prepared for the second day of operations (see map 6). Colonel Erulin issued orders to his units: the 1st Company was to move to the south along the route to Kapata; the 2d Company was to expand its positions to include more of the western half of the old town; and the 3d Company received instructions to clear Manika. While the 1st and 2d Companies had little contact with the rebels, the 3d Company was once more in a bitter fight with the FNLC.[14]

Captain Gausseres decided to take Manika in a pincer movement. The 1st Section under Lieutenant Bourgain was to move directly south into the quarter from its night position. Gausseres, with the rest of the 3d Company, would move east of the quarter and penetrate Manika from the flank to link up with Bourgain. Lieutenant Colonel Erulin had stressed speed in clearing the area and searching for hostages, and Gausseres hoped to catch the FNLC off guard. The company commander realized that the rebels' local militia, after retreating into Manika the previous day, had had ample opportunity to prepare its defenses.[15]

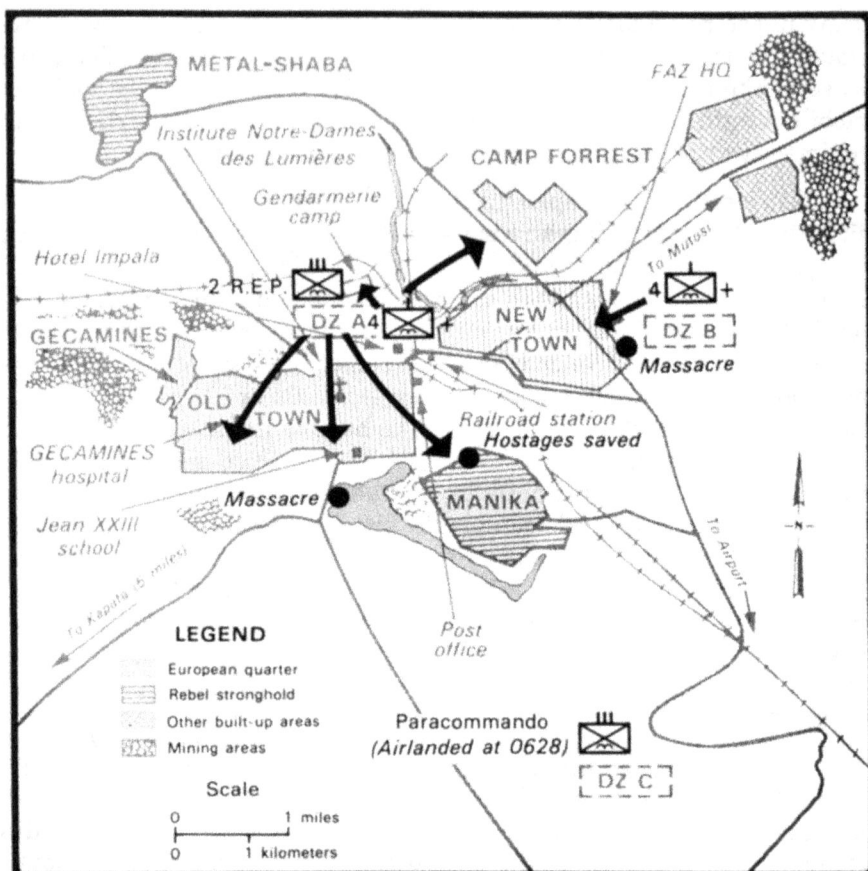

Map 6. Kolwezi, 20 May 1978

Bourgain's platoon moved off first. Easing along Avenue Okito, the 1st Section moved in bounds through the native quarter. In contrast with the European quarters of Kolwezi, Manika's streets were narrow and crooked, offering a defender excellent ambush positions. The rebels used the area to their advantage; less than 100 meters into the town, the Legionnaires began receiving fire. The shooting grew in intensity, and no matter how the lieutenant maneuvered his men, they made little progress. After an advance of about 200 meters, the 1st Section stopped and assumed defensive positions, and Bourgain radioed his company commander.[16]

Though not happy with the 1st Section's progress, Captain Gausseres could not complain too loudly. He was having his own problems just getting close to the native quarter. After moving off along the north side of the town at 0500, Gausseres had attempted to reach the railroad east of Manika. His unit drew rebel fire almost immediately. Though generally inaccurate, the rebel fire forced the Legionnaires to move slowly and cautiously. Consequently, the 3d Company did not reach the eastern entrance to the village until almost 0700. Halted 250 meters outside the town, Gausseres searched for a way to rout the rebels, who seemed perfectly willing to slug it out with the French. He had just decided to take the Protestant church on the outskirts of Manika when one of his men asked him to identify some troops approaching their rear. Turning to see, Gausseres swore, "Merde. Voilà, les Belges [Shit, there are the Belgians]!"[17]

After arising at 0400, the Belgian Paracommandos had quickly completed last-minute preparations for the day's mission. The first wave of eight C-130s took off at 0550 for Kolwezi. With Colonels Depoorter and Blume on board, the first C-130 led the formation in a low-level flight to the target. The first wave's initial flight of four C-130s with the 1st Para Battalion's lead elements swung in toward the target at 0628. Shuddering under the drag of full flaps, the C-130s slammed onto the runway, their rear ramps already lowering for the paras. Quickly, the men ran from the aircraft, the C-130s took off, and the next four C-130s swarmed in to repeat the operation. In minutes, the Belgians had 500 men on the ground.[18]

For the Paracommando Regiment, things were a bit confused initially. Briefed that the 311th Airborne Battalion had control of the field, the Belgians were at first surprised by the number of black soldiers present and by the variety of uniforms that made identification difficult. A less-disciplined unit might have opened fire and asked questions later, but the paras restrained their nervous fingers. Lieutenant Colonel Kesteloot, the regiment's deputy, sought out Major Mahele, the FAZ commander, and coordinated the field's defenses. Meanwhile, Depoorter ordered the 3d Para Battalion to move into the old town. Even as Major Couwenberg led his unit toward the city, the Belgians saw parachutes blossom northeast of Kolwezi.[19]

Following an uncomfortable evening waiting on the tarmac at Lubumbashi, the 2d R.E.P.'s second assault wave had boarded its aircraft shortly before dawn for the morning's jump. On board, Captain Grail's 4th Company was to jump on drop zone B and hit the new town from the rear. Meanwhile, the 2d R.E.P.'s reconnaissance section, mortar platoon, and main command post element were to jump on drop zone A. The reconnaissance section was to move on Camp Forrest and the old gendarmerie camp north of the city, and the mortar platoon was to establish firing positions on the drop zone to support the 2d R.E.P.'s operations.[20]

The drop went as planned, and the 4th Company assembled quickly. Captain Grail sent one section along his left flank to secure the FAZ command post. Another section moved to the right to take the Baron-Leveque building. Grail moved with that section and discovered the slaughterhouse missed by Gausseres the previous evening. Grail had just finished calling in the grim news when his men discovered Ms. Radu alive under a pile of bodies. Minutes later, the nearly starved Jurmann and Michel appeared from their hiding place in the ceiling, grateful for their apparent salvation. As the 4th Company secured the new town, the reconnaissance section took the police camp and Camp Forrest without trouble.[21]

Flying overhead in his C-160 command post, Colonel Gras was pleased so far with the morning's events. But his satisfaction turned to concern as he watched the Belgians conduct their assault on the airfield. When he saw the lead Belgian units head north to the town, he recognized that a dangerous situation was developing. With the arrival of his second wave, Colonel Depoorter had sent the 1st Para Battalion toward the new town. The entire Paracommando Regiment was marching toward Kolwezi. Gras flew over the field and attempted to stop the movement before the Belgians blundered into French positions. Gras was too late.[22]

Shortly after Captain Gausseres' 3d Company, 2d R.E.P., had spotted the approaching Belgians, he met the lead unit's commander, Captain De Wulf of the 17th Company, 3d Para Battalion, an old acquaintance. The two talked over their missions: De Wulf was there to evacuate the expatriates; Gausseres was attempting to expel the rebels from Manika. The two missions were completely different. Still, the two comrades parted amicably, each wishing the other success in his operation.[23]

The friendly atmosphere was short-lived. As the Belgians moved off and Gausseres returned his attention to Manika, firing broke out between the two European forces. Both sides had been under sporadic rebel fire, and neither knew the exact dispositions of the other. Each claimed it was the other that began the shooting. Fortunately, the firing was inaccurate as leaders on both sides brought their men under control before anyone got hurt. Aside from a residual mutual suspicion of each other's intent in the affair—a suspicion that still exists—the brief exchange of fire produced no casualties.[24]

Actually, the instance of friendly fire had positive effects on the remainder of the operation. With the failure of his attempt to halt the Belgian movement into the city via radio, Gras had his C-160 land on the airport. In his face-to-face meeting with the Belgians, Gras attempted to get Depoorter to halt the Belgian operation, a demand that Depoorter naturally refused. The differences in the two missions were apparent to both. Gras' mission was to drive rebels from the city; Depoorter's was to evacuate the foreign population. The Belgians did not care what happened to Kolwezi or Zaire once the operation was over as long as they did not leave anyone behind. Depoorter had only seventy-two hours to complete his operation, and he was ill-disposed to consider Gras' objections. Recognizing the futility of trying to change the Belgians' mission, Gras agreed to turn over the majority of the new and old towns to the Paracommando Regiment, leaving the central area of the city around the rail station and Manika to the 2d R.E.P. While the Belgians completed their evacuation with the FAZ and French airlift bolstering the 15th Wing, the 2d R.E.P. would continue to search the outlying districts for expatriates and rebels. At 0930, Depoorter reconfirmed the agreement with Erulin in the Hotel Impala.[25]

Though less than an ideal arrangement, the agreement was the first and only coordination between the two forces. Minimally, it stopped the Belgians and the French from shooting at one another. It also provided the 2d R.E.P. with needed medical support from the Paracommandos' surgical team. The French, in turn, placed their airlift at the disposal of the Belgian evacuation effort. That is not to say that relations between the two European neighbors were particularly cordial for the remainder of the operation. Gras and Erulin still did not like the Belgians' emphasis on a speedy evacuation of the expatriates. Gras felt the Belgians' haste had panicked the foreign population unnecessarily. Some of the French accused the Belgians of forcing the expatriates to leave. The Belgians felt the 2d R.E.P. was rather cavalier in its use of force against the locals. Belgian leaders reported that the French attempted to interfere with the Belgian operation. Both sides only grudgingly cooperated in coordinating patrols outside the city. Still, there was no further exchange of fire among the "friendly" forces in Kolwezi.[26]

In any case, the arrival of the Paracommando Regiment had not halted the activities of the 2d R.E.P. in clearing the city. After the exchange of fire between his 3d Company, 2d R.E.P., and the 3d Para Battalion, Captain Gausseres finally succeeded in reaching Lieutenant Bourgain's position. After a 2-hour fight to move the 900 meters to the 1st Section's location, Gausseres eased his company out of Manika, leaving it to be cleared later. That afternoon, the 2d R.E.P. got into the most serious fight of the operation when Erulin ordered the 4th Company to scout out the rail station at a village north of Metal-Shaba (see map 7). Captain Grail began the march at 1530 with his 3d Section in the lead. As the company closed on the objective, Grail ordered the 2d Section forward to check the village. Meanwhile, Chief Sergeant Cas of the 3d Section had climbed the station tower and reported spotting around 100 uniformed soldiers at the company's front.[27]

Grail had just refused Cas permission to open fire when the soldiers whom Grail thought were FAZ paras opened fire on the 3d Section. Grail soon found his company engaged by a heavy machine gun and 200 to 300 rebels. The 4th Company responded like veterans. Seeing the 3d Section under fire, the 2d Section set up a base of fire along a ridge northwest of its comrades. The 2d Section's snipers played havoc with the rebel machine gunners, killing them one by one as the FNLC attempted to man the gun. Still, it was not a one-way battle; rebel fire raked the 4th Company's positions killing Chief Sergeant Daniels and wounding Corporal Prudence. Grail saw that he would need help to clean out the area. After drawing back into a more defensible posture, Grail radioed Erulin and asked for reinforcements.[28]

Erulin responded immediately by ordering Captain Dubos' 2d Company to move to the village. "Bobosse" soon had his unit moving, mounted on Magirus trucks borrowed from the GECAMINES motor pool. With a Dutch mechanic who did not speak a word of French (he was known as "Godverdomme" by the Legionnaires due to his enthusiastic swearing) to guide it, the 2d Company arrived at Metal-Shaba quickly. Erulin's operations officer, Captain Coeveot, took command of the fight and directed the coordinated fire of the two companies and the newly arrived reconnaissance and mortar sections. The rebels broke under the assault and fled, harassed by a FAZ Mirage. Afterward, the French found that the FNLC had left behind nearly eighty dead. Aside from scattered firing during the evening, the struggle at Metal-Shaba ended the fighting around Kolwezi on 20 May.[29]

As the French concentrated on eliminating pockets of rebel resistance, the Paracommando Regiment focused on removing the foreign population from danger. By the morning of the 20th, at least sixty expatriate bodies had been found. By the time the evacuation was complete, some 160 expatriates and several hundred natives were

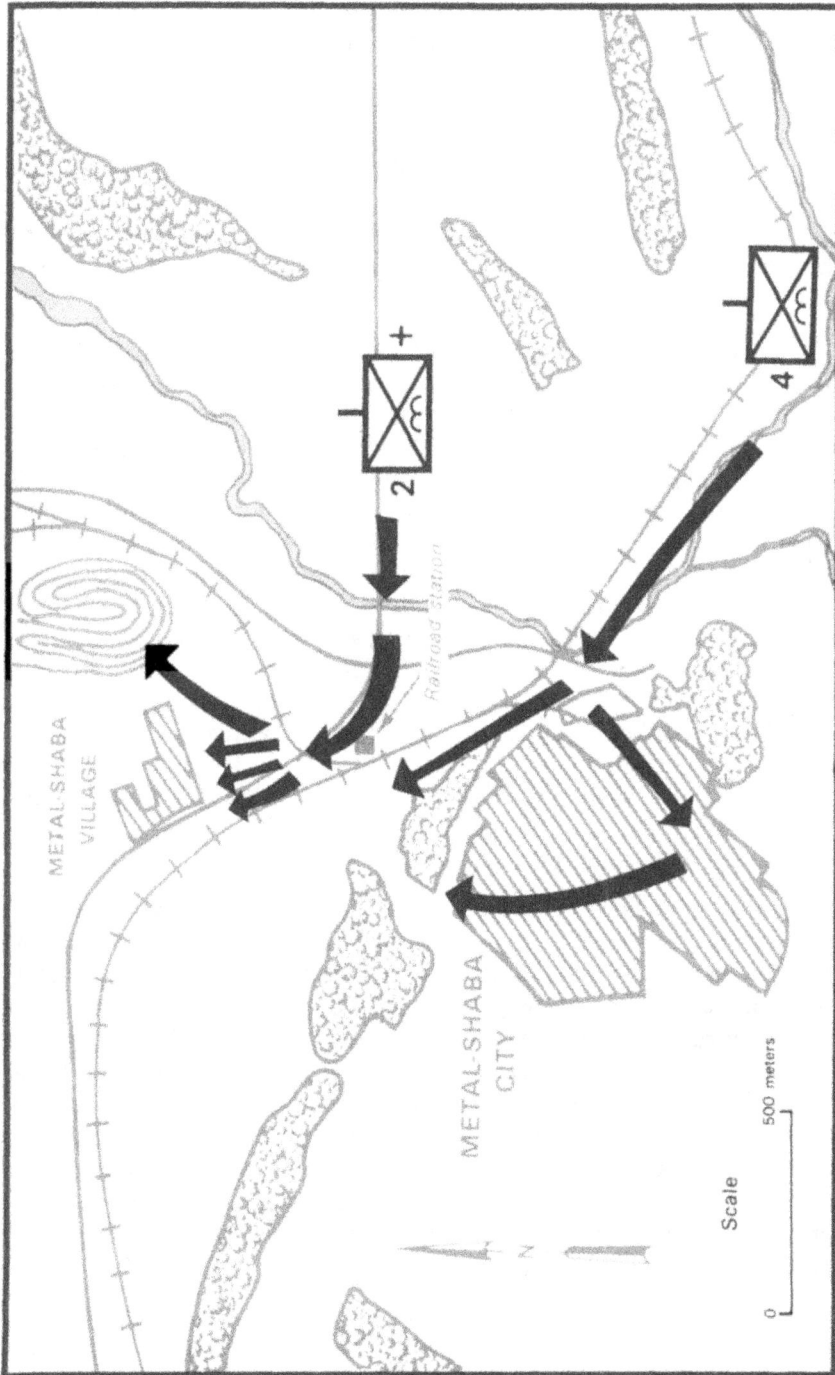

Map 7. Metal-Shaba

known to be dead. Kolwezi had been gutted—left without water, electricity, and food—and most of the survivors were more than willing to leave. Once the Belgians penetrated the city, the foreigners began gathering to depart, many in need of medical care. Some had seen their family members killed in front of them, and a fortunate few were reunited with loved ones who had been missing for several days. In any case, few asked to stay. One who asked the paras if the evacuation was mandatory was told, "Of course not! But, we won't be coming back next week either." The individual joined the refugees headed to the airport.[30]

At the airfield, the air traffic was moving the refugees out quickly. By 1230, some 500 expatriates had departed for Kamina, where the Belgians had established an intermediate processing center. Around midday, a Royal Air Force VC-10 flying hospital arrived from the United Kingdom via Lusaka, Zambia. As Italy's contribution to the evacuation, an Italian C-130 flew in with additional spare parts for the 15th Wing. The U.S. Air Force's C-141s continued to ferry fuel and supplies into Kamina and Lubumbashi to keep the operation going. That afternoon, President Mobutu flew in to compliment the French and Belgians on the operation. Taken to visit the massacre site in the new town, the shocked dictator gasped, "My God, they have smashed their heads in." He soon departed for Kinshasa. At dusk, the Belgians rounded up abandoned vehicles and lined the runways with them, using their headlights to illuminate the field. By the end of the operations on the 20th, the 15th Wing and others had flown 1,100 paras into Kolwezi and evacuated some 2,000 expatriates. They continued the operation the following day.[31]

After the drama of 19 and 20 May, 21 May proved almost anticlimactic for the Paracommando Regiment. The Belgians dispatched motorized patrols in company strength to areas as far as forty kilometers away. One patrol made visual contact with rebels fleeing toward the border, but no shots were exchanged. The Belgian ambassador, Rittweger de Moore, flew in from Kinshasa and toured the area with Depoorter and Blume. Significantly, the ambassador suggested that some of the paras might stay behind once the withdrawal began. Mobutu paid yet another visit to the city that afternoon, stopping briefly to see the Paracommandos. By late afternoon, Depoorter was able to report that Operation Red Bean was virtually over.[32]

In Kolwezi, the situation was virtually the same for the 2d R.E.P. That morning, the French ambassador, Ross, had visited the city and toured it with Colonels Gras and Erulin. Ross also brought word that

Mobutu, his command C-130 in the background, is briefed by Colonel
Depoorter on the mission and execution of operations on 20 May

the French might be required to extend their stay in Shaba as the
rapid flight of the expatriates from Kolwezi had spread panic
throughout the province. The 2d R.E.P. had continued to concentrate
on cleaning out Manika, where it was believed the rebels had once
again left stay-behind supporters along with weapons and
ammunition. That day, the unit's vehicles were driven in from
Lubumbashi where they had arrived via U.S. airlift. More good news
came in with the return of the 2d R.E.P.'s antitank gunners, missing
since the drop on the 19th. During a visit at 1600, Mobutu instructed
Gras to assume command of all friendly forces in Kolwezi, a decision
hardly palatable to the Belgians. Nevertheless, by the end of the day,
the French were able to report that rebel activity around Kolwezi had
ceased.[33]

With the arrival of its vehicles, the 2d R.E.P. prepared to expand
its operations outside the city. After debriefing the refugees, Erulin
began dispatching a series of motorized patrols the next day to cut off
rebel escape routes. Rumors were rampant that the FNLC had
withdrawn with up to seventy expatriate hostages, and Erulin still
had hopes of saving the French military advisers who had disappeared
in the rebels' initial attack. On 22 May, the 2d R.E.P. mounted an
action to Kapata, ten kilometers from Kolwezi. Capturing several
rebels and killing four, the Legionnaires failed to find any hostages.
Erulin's men carried out similar missions on 23, 25, and 26 May, and
although these missions succeeded in killing several rebels, they failed
to find any more hostages. Nor were they without cost to the 2d R.E.P.,

Refugees waiting to board a C-130

which lost three men killed in action after 21 May. Nevertheless, the 2d R.E.P.'s combat in Shaba was over by 27 May, when the first company departed for Lubumbashi and its ultimate return to Corsica on 6 June. In eight days, the 2d R.E.P. had captured 163 rebels, killed around 252, and seized an enormous amount of military hardware. The cost had not been cheap: the 2d R.E.P. lost five dead and another twenty-five wounded.[34]

Ironically, the Belgian Paracommando Regiment, so reluctantly dispatched to Zaire by Brussels, was on hand to witness the French departure. On 22 May, following the end of the air evacuation the previous day, the Paracommando Regiment began its withdrawal from Kolwezi. At 0400, word arrived from Brussels ordering Depoorter to pull back to Kamina, and the 3d Para Battalion boarded the aircraft almost immediately. In 55 hours in Kolwezi, the Paracommando Regiment had evacuated 2,300 civilians without a single casualty. By 1000, the 3d Para had closed on Kamina and the 1st Para was on its way. At 1325, Depoorter reported that the entire unit was at Kamina prepared to return to Belgium. Unknown to the paras, not all would be going home right away. At 1800, a message arrived from Brussels congratulating the regiment on its performance and directing Depoorter to leave one battalion behind in Shaba. The next morning at 0400, the 1st Para Battalion and the antitank company watched the rest of the regiment board planes to fly home.[35]

With the current state of uneasiness in Shaba—especially among the foreign population—the Belgian government had agreed with Ambassador de Moor's assessment that some form of stabilizing force would be needed. With the FAZ already openly pillaging Kolwezi, it was clear that Zaire's own armed forces were still ineffective. Discussions were already under way in Washington, Paris, and Brussels concerning a return of the Moroccans or some other African security force. At this stage, an interim security force was needed, and the task fell to the Paracommando Regiment. The 1st Para Battalion, reinforced with additional mortars, logistical and medical support, and airlift, was to assure the safety of the expatriates in other Shaba towns. Prohibited from assisting the FAZ in any actions, the 1st Para Battalion remained in the country until 25 June when the 3d Para Battalion returned. The 3d Para stayed until the arrival of the Inter-African Force in July. Though the Inter-African Force would remain in Zaire for the next few months, the Second Shaba War was over.[36]

Although the war was over, its reverberations were only beginning. The invasion was a blow the staggering Zairian economy could ill afford. The attack had shut down the country's mining industry, and within a week, the world price for cobalt jumped 24 percent. With Zaire already $3 billion in debt, Mobutu's Western supporters quickly raised $100 million to forestall a total Zairian collapse. Economic measures aside, Mobutu faced other problems. In contrast to the euphoria after Mobutu's "victory" in the eighty-day war, the atmosphere in Zaire was almost funereal after the Kolwezi disaster. Once again, the FAZ carried out reprisals against the Shaban population, and the fear of repression spread as far as Kinshasa. This time, however, Mobutu's backers stepped in and forced reform measures on the recalcitrant dictator. If he wanted to continue to receive Western economic aid, he was going to have to take real steps to control the corruption in Zaire's government. Grudgingly, Mobutu complied, even going so far as to release a number of political prisoners jailed in the aftermath of Shaba I.[37]

The other half of the bargain for Mobutu to receive Western aid was for him to settle his differences with Neto of Angola. When Mobutu made disturbing remarks at the Franco-African Summit at the end of May about American corruption in government, U.S. Secretary of State Cyrus Vance warned him to stop interfering in Angolan affairs or he would face yet another Shaba invasion. Negotiations between the two African neighbors had begun before the invasion was even over and had progressed well, producing a Neto promise to disarm the FNLC. Following another round of meetings in Brazzaville, Mobutu and Neto agreed to quit supporting groups hostile to the other's regime. The honeymoon was capped with a visit by Neto to Kinshasa in August. Still, the episode ended with observers wondering how Neto was going to handle the FNLC, Mobutu, or the

U.S. Secretary of State Cyrus Vance warned Mobutu to stop interfering in Angolan affairs

tribal hatreds that remained in Shaba. As one Moroccan officer, newly arrived as a member of the Inter-African Force, put it, "I was here last year, I am here now, and I have no doubt that I will be back again next year."38

While Mobutu's Western supporters were telling him to get along with his neighbors, they engaged in their own squabbles. The principal dispute was, as might be expected, between France and Belgium. France, and d'Estaing in particular, had emerged from the crisis with a strong measure of support for the intervention among Europe's news media, especially that of Belgium. In contrast, the Belgian press had been vocal in criticizing the Tindemans government for its sluggish handling of the affair. In response to that heckling and the French remarks about the disclosure of the Paracommandos' movement, the Belgian government had accused France of neocolonialism and of exploitation of the crisis for economic gain. Belgian observers referred to the 2d R.E.P.'s action as another example of "d'Estaing's Africa Corps." Watching from the sidelines and ever hopeful of manipulating the situation to his own ends, Mobutu threatened to replace all Belgian workers with French workers, a threat Brussels felt sure had originated in Paris. Tindemans, however, managed to reduce the tension appreciably with an unscheduled trip to Paris in late May. Meeting with d'Estaing and Mobutu, the three resolved some of the differences brought out by Shaba II.39

Across the Atlantic, one of Mobutu's more reluctant allies also struggled with the aftershocks of Shaba II. Following the Carter administration's decision to alert the 82d Airborne Division, the news media had been aware of the message being sent to the Soviets vis-à-vis the crisis in Zaire. Having served notice that it would react to perceived threats in the Third World, the Carter administration waited until the French had intervened and then canceled the 82d's alert, a step made possible by the Morris-Knudsen evacuation.[40]

Yet White House advisers, concerned over the administration's poor standing in the press, convinced President Carter to be aggressive in his pronouncements to the press rather than low key as in the previous year. Carter came out blasting—and promptly shot himself in the foot over the question of Cuban involvement in Shaba II. After the Ford administration's embarrassment over the Angolan fiasco in 1975–76, Carter's advisers had treated the 1977 Shaba invasion as strictly an African affair. But things had changed by 1978 with the growing insurgency in Rhodesia, supported by the Soviets and the Red Chinese, and the massive intervention by the Soviets and Cubans in the Ethiopian-Somali conflict. President Carter's advisers had convinced him that he had to draw the line somewhere and that the Shaba province was the place to do so. Unfortunately, the president's charges of direct Cuban involvement rang empty when U.S. congressional leaders asked to see hard evidence to support the accusations. In the end, many observers were more inclined to believe Castro's claims that he had tried to forestall the invasion and had gone so far as to warn the United States that it was coming. Concerned over bolstering his image as a tough international statesman, President Carter had picked the wrong arena and, in the end, only appeared incompetent to Congress and the news media.[41]

So, almost as quickly as it began, the Second Shaba War ended. As in 1964 after the U.S.-Belgian intervention, the reverberations of the crisis had a greater effect outside the country of Zaire than they did within the Mobutu regime. Like the crises of 1964 or 1977, the 1978 invasion ended on a note of doubt, doubt that anything lasting or beneficial had taken place. Once again, the government in Kinshasa had survived another challenge due largely to external support. And, once again, those who had provided the support came away with burned fingers and the nagging suspicion it would not be the last time Mobutu called for help.

VIII. CONCLUSIONS

In reviewing the operations in Kolwezi, clearly French and Belgian political differences dictated their conduct of separate military efforts. Under the guidance of President Giscard d'Estaing, France pursued a policy intended to reinforce its continued interest in Africa. Although largely a military program designed to bolster the African countries against Soviet-Cuban or other forms of communism, France's activist policy included economic dimensions, as d'Estaing intended to expand France's commercial status on the continent. Though Belgium had given Zaire (the Congo) its independence in 1960, Belgian economic ties to the country had remained strong, so strong in fact that Belgium tended to regard the former colony as its economic fiefdom. With the French response to the Shaba I crisis and Mobutu's clumsy threats to replace Belgian interests with French, the Belgians were loathe to participate in a combined operation with their European neighbors.

The Belgians were equally reluctant to consider a unilateral intervention in Zaire. Memories of the 1960s were fresh in Belgian minds. More Westerners had died after the 1964 rescues and subsequent withdrawal than before. Since Shaba I had turned out to be more a comic opera than a war, the Belgian cabinet futilely hoped that the rebels would not harm the Westerners captured in Kolwezi. Prime Minister Leo Tindemans' handling of the crisis reflected this hesitation. Forming a special crisis cabinet that excluded opposition parties, the Belgian cabinet attempted indirect negotiations with the FNLC to evacuate the expatriates. An agreement that military action was unavoidable only came after the killings had begun in Kolwezi. Once that decision was reached, the Belgian government retained tight control over the operation.

In contrast, the French considered intervention from the very beginning of the war. Certainly, France had demonstrated a willingness to intervene in conflicts on the continent, as shown in Chad, Lebanon, or Djibouti. President d'Estaing's activist policy demanded such actions in order to remain credible. When the Kolwezi crisis began, d'Estaing did not bother with a crisis cabinet. Instead, he worked with an emergency task force formed from government technicians. Matching this proactive approach, d'Estaing had the indefatigable Colonel Gras in Kinshasa to push for the intervention. Once the French had decided on action, d'Estaing turned the operation over to Gras for execution, a step that would have been inconceivable from the Belgian perspective.

Equally inconceivable was the French cooperation with the Zairian armed forces. After Shaba I, France had become Zaire's principal supplier of arms and training. Moreover, French military teams conducted much of this training inside Zaire and worked directly with FAZ units. As in the case of Lieutenant Colonel Ballade's advisers to the 311th Airborne Battalion, the associations became quite close. In planning to retake Kolwezi, Gras had intended to establish a combined French-Zairian brigade to drive overland from Lubumbashi. Unfortunately, Mobutu had destroyed any chance to conduct the operation as he wasted the FAZ units that were available. When the French deployed the 2d R.E.P., the FAZ provided the C-130 crews—unskilled as they were—and other support never offered to the Belgians. French pilots manned FAZ Mirages to fly combat missions against the rebels, and the French advisers rejoined the remnants of the 311th. Mobutu completed the cooperative effort by placing all the FAZ troops in Kolwezi under Gras' command. In contrast to the free hand given Gras by Paris, the Belgian government placed tight restrictions on Colonel Depoorter's cooperation with the FAZ in order to avoid compromising his mission, even after the Kolwezi operation ended.

An examination of the two forces' missions captures the fundamental differences between them. France's policy toward Africa was clearly activist; d'Estaing made it clear that France would not tolerate further Communist adventurism on the continent. Erulin's mission, while equally activist, was to restore order in Kolwezi until the Zairian armed forces could assume responsibility for the area. By driving the rebels out of Kolwezi and Shaba, the French felt the Westerners could be saved and the stability of Zaire maintained.

On the other hand, Belgium had no intention of getting involved with propping up the shaky Zairian government. The memories of the disastrous Katangan secession and the 1960 and 1964 interventions were too strong for Brussels to forget. The Paracommando Regiment returned to Zaire in 1978 to conduct an operation similar to the one conducted in Stanleyville (Kisangani) in 1964. Depoorter's mission was to rescue the foreign population with a minimum of force. That did not mean the Belgians were forbidden to use their weapons; the paras were fully prepared to kill if the situation had required it. Depoorter's rules of engagement allowed him to use force against anyone who attempted to interfere with the safe evacuation of the expatriates— including the French if necessary.

Just as the squabbling between France and Belgium over Zaire caused political problems, it drastically affected the military operations meant to resolve the situation. For a fleeting moment, there had been a chance for a truly combined and coordinated operation to rescue the foreign population in Kolwezi. With the realization by both Paris and Brussels that an intervention was unavoidable, the Belgian and French planners in Kinshasa met to coordinate their operations. The 2d R.E.P. and the Paracommando Regiment would have conducted a combined airborne operation on 20 May. Yet the announcement by Brussels that Belgian and French military forces were on the alert to deploy to Zaire ended any hope for further cooperation. Angered and alarmed by the Belgian disclosure of an imminent operation, the French government pushed Gras to move up the date of the 2d R.E.P.'s operation.

Colonel Gras' decision to accede to Paris' request to advance the date of Operation Leopard accounted for much of the French operation's hastiness. In fact, the 2d R.E.P.'s quick response was a result of the French colonel's foresight in planning the operation before Paris had even made a decision to act. As Erulin got off the plane in Kinshasa, the French Military Mission provided him with a nearly complete plan that he used with few changes. From that point on, most of the 2d R.E.P.'s problems could be attributed to bad luck or "the fog of war."

The French were forced to accept the risks in mounting the operation on the 19th. Certainly, Gras recognized the need to parachute in close to the city in order to secure all of it quickly, as well as the need for air support to make the operation feasible. He had wanted to get both waves on the ground as rapidly as possible to conduct the operation. After all, the 2d R.E.P. had only some 600 men to fight several thousand rebels. But both Gras and Erulin realized that the expatriates were in grave danger due to the announcements in the world news media that the French and the Belgians were going to intervene. As Erulin later explained, "All the initial phase was becoming more and more based on bluff and rapid action: for this reason the order went out to the units to regroup as rapidly as possible to get to their initial objectives without regards to casualties."[1]

The French accepted more than just the risk of friendly casualties. The airborne operation, with its unskilled crews, ill-maintained aircraft, and overloaded troops, courted disaster. Jumping in marginal conditions with ill-matched equipment and unfamiliar parachutes, the 2d R.E.P. suffered remarkably few casualties from the jump, a fortunate circumstance since Erulin had been forced to mount the operation with inadequate medical support. Furthermore, the Legionnaires began the operation after almost forty-eight hours without sleep, and they continued to operate for another two days before getting any appreciable rest. To meet the challenge, Erulin relied heavily on the special training and character of his unit.

To understand Gras' and Erulin's calm acceptance of the enormous tasks facing the 2d R.E.P., one need only look at the unit's background. By reputation, the French Foreign Legion did not attract those who possessed gentle souls. The 2d R.E.P. carried on the tradition of the Foreign Legion parachute regiments that were so active in the Indochina and Algerian wars. This jump into Kolwezi was the 2d R.E.P.'s first combat jump since the unit had been destroyed in Vietnam at Dien Bien Phu, a fact that gave the unit a certain élan when it came to facing the tall odds at Kolwezi. Although the 2d R.E.P. did not go to Kolwezi to conduct "a Western" shoot-out (as reported by certain Belgian critics), Erulin's men had a certain hardness of attitude not often found in peacetime.[2]

Aside from its reputation and morale, the 2d R.E.P. was an extremely well-trained unit. Since Erulin's men had practiced this type of mission many times, the concept was familiar to them. With a high level of training in basic infantry skills, the Legionnaires were able to adapt to the changing situation. After the extremely confused jump on the 19th, the men assembled and took their initial objectives, fighting off attacks that included armored cars. By using night patrols, ambushes, and listening posts, the Legionnaires disrupted rebel activities that first night in Kolwezi. Their specialty training also paid dividends, especially that of sniper training. Coupled with their mission's intent to kill the rebels, the offensive use of the unit's snipers allowed the 2d R.E.P. to maintain the upper hand against a sometimes determined resistance. So, in accepting the risks of this operation, Colonels Gras and Erulin counted heavily on the abilities of the men in the 2d R.E.P.[3]

Matching the abilities of the 2d R.E.P., the Belgian Paracommando Regiment was also an elite unit. Colonel Depoorter's Paracommandos, like Erulin's Legionnaires, were proud of their unit's history. Unlike the 2d R.E.P., however, that pride came from their success in past operations, not from a heritage of glorious defeat. The difference is critical in understanding the Belgians' approach to the operation. Even in 1964, in the Dragon Rouge operation in Stanleyville when the paras were told to consider all blacks as enemies, the regiment had been selective in its use of force against the Simba rebels. In 1978, the Paracommando Regiment modeled its operations in Kolwezi after this experience.

The Paracommando Regiment applied a number of the lessons it learned in 1964 to its Kolwezi operation. Because of the 1964 experience, Colonel Depoorter intended to seize the city as rapidly as possible rather than secure the airport as his initial objective. Depoorter decided to conduct an air assault operation so that his assembly after airlanding would allow for a more rapid penetration of the city than an airdrop. The paras' experience in 1964 had shown that the delay required for assembly after an airborne operation could be fatal for any hostages waiting for rescue.

Another lesson learned by the Belgians from the 1978 operation was to include a fully mobile surgical unit. After the earlier Congo operations, the Belgians had pushed for the creation of such a unit to support operations where civilian or military casualties might be suffered far from an adequate surgical facility. According to French after-action reports, several 2d R.E.P. lives were saved because the Belgians had included a surgical team in the Kolwezi operation.

Providing organic mobility for such operations was another lesson learned from the 1964 experience, when the paras had relied heavily on the availability of abandoned cars to mount their operations. In 1978, the Belgian regiment took its organic transport to Kolwezi and, from the first day of its operations, was able to dispatch patrols outside the city. The French, on their part, noted in reports that they relied on confiscated transport and bemoaned the need for organic transport in the 2d R.E.P.'s operation.

In contrast, however, the Belgian political leaders failed to grasp a major lesson of 1964: the impossibility of conducting an operation in conjunction with another military operation without effective coordination. The Belgian defense minister's orders for Depoorter to avoid all contact with the French were absolutely absurd. In 1964, a similar situation had developed with the coordination between the Paracommando Regiment and the ground column under Colonel Frédéric J. L. A. Vandewalle. Then, as in 1978, the paras were conducting a humanitarian rescue, and the Vandewalle column was on a mission to restore governmental control. In order to avoid conflict between the two Belgian-led elements, coordination before the operation and after the arrival of Vandewalle's force proved to be necessary. The same need was present in 1978, and the failure to coordinate the two operations ended in a near disastrous firefight between the Belgians and the French. Just as it had been in 1964, the reluctance to conduct the required liaison in 1978 was due to political restrictions that were not fully thought out.

Apart from these operational lessons, certain other fundamentals from the 1978 operations are evident. A crisis situation can develop rapidly in Third World countries, and the developments may be beyond the normal intelligence focus of Western countries. Zaire, so often the scene of previous eruptions of violence, still caught Western intelligence agencies off guard. In contrast to 1964 when the United States and Belgium spent months sifting through and agonizing over the available information, the 1978 situation in Kolwezi occurred rapidly, leaving little time for reflection. Even acquiring maps can be a problem, and in a fast-moving situation like the one in Kolwezi, there may not be time to request maps or to conduct aerial photography.

Another issue is that in today's world, there are no poorly armed insurgents. In 1978, the FNLC had modern weapons, including armored cars, and the French found out that the rebels knew how to use them. Modern arms and the training to use them are readily available on the world market. Therefore, modern reaction forces, such as light infantry, must be prepared to deal with determined, well-trained foes. Furthermore, intelligence officers must be careful in assessing probable reactions by insurgent forces such as the FNLC. One cannot assume, as Brussels did in 1978, that such a force will adhere to international conventions. Today, it is safer to assume the opposite. The same holds true in assessing military capabilities; the nature and potency of military units must be carefully evaluated.[4]

Reacting to a hostage or evacuation situation places special demands on units. First, these situations usually develop rapidly, generally without warning. Therefore, units tasked with such missions have little time to prepare and no time to train. Often, such missions may require that hostages be rescued at the same time other refugees are being evacuated. Consequently, specially trained units charged with rescuing hostages may have to coordinate their operations with the more conventional forces conducting the evacuation. Thus, such cooperation should be rehearsed in training. Once an alert goes out, there is little time for practice; it is truly a "come-as-you-are" environment.

In addition, such operations demand special communications, such as the Paracommandos used in talking directly to their national authorities. By their very nature, hostage rescue missions are heavily political, and liaison with the diplomatic mission in the country and the news media is mandatory. The Belgians had adequate measures prepared along these lines, but the French did not. As Erulin reported afterward, his staff was almost overwhelmed with the need to coordinate diplomatic and press functions. All these requirements dictate that units that might face such contingency missions should train to conduct them—as the Paracommando Regiment did.[5]

Tied to the ability to fight rebels (such as the FNLC of 1978) is the ability to deploy forces to the combat zone. Often, the logistical requirements of even light infantry forces such as the 2d R.E.P. and the Paracommando Regiment are underestimated by those who superficially examine potential operations in places like Zaire. After the 1964 experience, the Belgians developed austere area logistical packages to support any further operations along similar lines; the French after-action reports noted that such logistical packages would have served their force well in Kolwezi.

To deploy and support the Belgian Paracommando Regiment, the 15th Wing flew 32 round-trip and 426 local C-130 missions—1,726 hours of flying time. In a sixty-hour period covering 19 to 21 May, the Belgian crews flew forty-three C-130 and fourteen Boeing 727 missions, with some of the crews logging thirty hours of flight time. With an additional 210 flying hours on its Boeing 727s, the 15th Wing still needed the assistance of Sabena, with 10 airliners, and the U.S. Air Force, with 8 C-141s, to complete its operations (with support not included in the above totals).

Aside from airframes and crews, the 15th Wing also needed austere base maintenance packages to keep its operation going. During the operations at Kamina, the 15th Wing's mechanics completed four engine changes at the central African base and another five back in Belgium. The same staggering requirements proved necessary to support the 2d R.E.P. Even using the five FAZ C-130s and three French C-160s in Zaire, the 2d R.E.P. required five airliners and two additional C-160s to deploy its men. To transport the 2d R.E.P.'s equipment, the French needed twenty C-141s and one C-5. All this airlift was needed to deploy some 2,000 "light infantry" to Zaire to evacuate 2,300 expatriates to Europe.[6]

The operations to retake Kolwezi in 1978 should not be dismissed as something unusual or unlikely to reoccur, nor should they be discounted as European operations of little interest to U.S. planners. Even though the United States did not commit ground troops to the operation, the 82d Airborne Division had some 2,000 paratroops on alert at one stage of the crisis. Moreover, in the months following the crisis in Kolwezi, American troops found themselves on alert for rescue or evacuation operations in Iran, followed by the disaster at Desert One. Since those operations, U.S. forces have been committed to similar operations in Lebanon, Grenada, Sudan, Somalia, Liberia, Panama, and the Persian Gulf. Without doubt, U.S. forces will conduct further ventures. Thus, the French and Belgian operations of 1978 have special relevance.

APPENDIX A

Personalities, Terms, and Acronyms

Personalities

Zairian

General Babia

FAZ chief of staff in 1978 who had the situation under control.

Joseph Kasavubu

Ineffective president of the Democratic Republic of the Congo from 1960 to 1965.

Patrice Lumumba

First prime minister of the Congo whose flamboyance in office helped set off the violence of the early 1960s in the Congo. He died while a captive of Tshombe. A martyr, he became a rallying point for all with a grudge against the central government.

Major Mahele

Commanding officer of the 311th Airborne Battalion who had the dubious honor of selecting one of his companies as a sacrifice to Mobutu's ego. His performance in reaching Kolwezi was outstanding.

General Nathaniel Mbumba

One-time police chief of Katanga province. After Mobutu's revenge against the Lunda and the ex-gendarmes in Katanga following the 1967 revolt, he crossed into Angola and became the military head of the FNLC.

President Mobutu Sese Seko

"President" of Zaire since seizing power in 1965. He was corrupt and difficult to deal with as the leader of Africa's potentially wealthiest country and responsible for Zaire's miserable economic status. As the self-styled leader of Zaire's armed forces, he has rewarded success with exile or worse. Formerly known as Joseph Mobutu before Zairianizing his name, he is also known as "Le Guide [the guide]" or "Citoyen [citizen]."

Moise Tshombe

Former "president" of the Katangan seccession against the Congo's central government who was responsible for the formation of the Katanga Gendarmerie. After a year's exile, he returned to the Congo in 1964 to become prime minister and defeat the Simba Rebellion. He was exiled again in 1965.

Angolan

Agostino Neto

Leader of the MPLA who won the civil war to control Angola. He also sponsored the FNLC in revenge for Mobutu's support for the FNLA.

Holden Roberto	Leader of the FNLA who received Mobutu's aid in the 1975–76 war for Angola. Aided by the United States, Roberto lost his bid for power.
Jonas Savimbi	Leader of UNITA who was loosely allied with Roberto in the 1975 war. He continues to fight against Neto and his Cuban supporters.

Belgian

Colonel Alaine Blume	Commanding officer, 15th Wing, who flew the first aircraft into Kolwezi on 20 May 1978.
Paul Vanden Boeynants	Belgian defense minister who claimed that the news releases on the French and Belgian movements were necessary so the FNLC would know that the units were to evacuate the foreigners not attack the rebels.
Colonel Henri J. G. ("Rik") Depoorter	Commanding officer, Belgian Paracommando Regiment, who had his entire regiment on the way to Zaire within thirty hours of the alert. His original plan was a more effective version of what the French did on 19 May 1978.
Jean Schramme	Belgian planter in Katanga province who became a mercenary during the Katangan secession and formed his own unit, the Leopard Battalion. After the secession failed, he crossed into Angola. He returned to fight the Simbas in 1964, fought the rebellion of 1966, and led the rebellion of 1967.
Henri Simonet	The Belgian foreign minister who held off from intervention until requests from the Belgian mission in Zaire made action unavoidable.
Leo Tindemans	Belgian prime minister whose government's handling of the crisis caused an uproar in the Belgian press.
Colonel Frédéric J. L. A. Vandewalle	Belgian chief of security in the Congo during the colonial period. With Tshombe's secession, he served as the Belgian consul in Katanga and oversaw the creation of the gendarmerie. After Tshombe's return to the Congo in 1964, Vandewalle returned to create a combined Belgian, mercenary, and Katangan outfit to defeat the Simbas.

French

Lieutenant Colonel Phillipe Erulin	Commanding officer, 2d R.E.P., who executed an unfamiliar plan twenty-four hours ahead of schedule.
President Giscard d'Estaing	French president whose activist approach to the Soviets' gains in Africa led to French support of Mobutu in 1977 and the intervention in 1978. Critics dubbed the actions as evidence of d'Estaing's "Africa Corps."

	Once he made the decision to act in 1978, he allowed his subordinates to do their jobs.
Colonel Yves Gras	Commander of the French Military Mission who was responsible for the drive to get the French to intervene in Kolwezi. He convinced Ambassador Ross to go on record in support of the intervention. He also had the foresight to begin planning the operation before the decision to intervene had been made and designed the parameters of the plan.
René Jorniac	President d'Estaing's adviser on African affairs who, after turning down Gras' suggestion for an intervention, ended up calling Gras and asking him to intervene ahead of schedule.
Colonel Larzul	French military attaché who worked closely with Gras in planning the operation. He jumped on the second wave of the airdrop.
André Ross	The French ambassador in Zaire who got on well with his military staff. He strongly favored a military intervention.

American

Jimmy Carter	U.S. president who virtually ignored the 1977 invasion. His attempt to play on Cuban involvement in 1978 backfired.
Zbigniew Brzezinski	President Carter's national security adviser who encouraged Carter to react in 1978 to the Soviet-Cuban gains on the African continent.
Cyrus Vance	U.S. secretary of state in 1978 who knew Mobutu from the 1964 crisis. In 1978, he warned Mobutu to behave or Shaba III was just around the corner.
Andrew Young	U.S. ambassador to the United Nations who tried to keep the Carter administration's focus in Africa on the question of apartheid. In 1977, he succeeded, but in 1978, he failed.

Terms

Zairian

Brazzaville Accords	Agreement made in 1977 between Mobutu and Neto to cease support for each other's dissident groups. Mobutu's failure to comply led to Shaba II.
Colombe	Code name for the FNLC's attack on Kolwezi.
Katangan Gendarmerie	Mercenary-led forces created under the guidance of Belgian officers under Colonel Vandewalle. The Katangan Gendarmerie fought UN forces to a standstill

until they received more support. After the Katangan secession, the gendarmes went into exile in Angola. Returning in 1964 at the behest of Tshombe, the gendarmes, again led by Vandewalle's Belgians and mercenaries, helped put down the Simba Rebellion. After the 1966 and 1967 mercenary rebellions, the gendarmes returned to Angola. (See FNLC.)

Kaymanyola Division	The "elite" FAZ unit that protected Kolwezi.
Simbas	Members of a rebel movement that revolted against the central government in 1964. The Simba movement was based on superstition and discontent. They took two-thirds of the Congo before they were defeated by a Belgian-American-Zairian coalition. The Simba seizure of Stanleyville and the holding of 2,000 hostages led to the Dragon operations.
Zairianization	Mobutu's program of "authenticity," meant to break all colonial ties by renaming everyone and everything that had a Western or colonial-associated name. Under this program, the Congo became Zaire.

Belgian

Dragon operations	Dragon Rouge—the Belgian-American airborne operation to take Stanleyville on 24 November 1964.
	Dragon Noir—the rescue at Paulis on 26 November 1964.
Red Bean	Code word for the 1978 Belgian operation at Kolwezi.
Samaritan	The Belgian plan to evacuate expatriates from Shaba in 1977 (Shaba I).

French

Bonité	The final name given to Operation Leopard by the French General Staff.
Leopard	The original code word for the French intervention in Kolwezi.

Other

Morris-Knudsen	American engineering firm that had its base camp northwest of Kolwezi.

Acronyms

ANC	Armée Nationale Congolaise—name of the Democratic Republic of the Congo's armed forces after

independence. It was formerly the Force Publique under Belgian colonial rule. (See FAZ.)

FAZ	Forces Armées Zairois—the ANC's new name in 1974 (which did not make it any better).
FLEC	Front for the Liberation of the Cabinda Enclave—the Angolan opposition group supported by Mobutu.
FNLA	National Front for the Liberation of Angola—the Angolan insurgent organization led by Holden Roberto and supported by Mobutu and the United States. It was defeated in the Angolan Civil War and still maintained bases in Zaire in 1977.
FNLC	Front for the National Liberation of the Congo—the Katangan Gendarmerie's adopted political title under General Mbumba. The FNLC allied itself with Neto's MPLA in Angola and launched the Shaba invasions in 1977 and 1978.
FODELICO	Democratic Forces for the Liberation of the Congo—the opposition group formed in 1974 around survivors of the 1964 rebellion.
FSA	African Socialist Forces—an opposition group formed in 1964 after the fall of Stanleyville to government forces.
GECAMINES	See UMHK.
MARC	Action Movement for the Resurrection of the Congo—the opposition party formed as a breakaway from the MPR in 1974.
MMF	French Military Mission.
MNLC	National Movement for the Liberation of the Congo—a Marxist-Leninist group formed in 1965.
MPLA	Popular Movement for the Liberation of Angola—an Angolan insurgent organization led by Agostino Neto. Helped by the Cubans and the FNLC, the MPLA defeated its opposition to win control of Angola.
MPR	Popular Movement of the Revolution—Mobutu's party, created in the late 1960s. Under the MPR's platform, Mobutu pushed through the laws making him a virtual dictator.
OAU	Organization of African Unity.
PRP	People's Revolutionary Party—another post-1964 opposition group that remained a disaster in the field.
UMHK	Union Minière du Haut-Katanga—nationalized by Mobutu in 1966, which became the Générale Congolaise des Minerais (GECOMIN), then rechartered

with a new agreement with the Belgians as Générale des Carrières et des Mines (GECAMINES) in 1971. The GECAMINES was the principal employee of the expatriates in Kolwezi.

UNITA
National Union for the Total Independence of Angola—Angolan insurgents led by Jonas Savimbi, who were sometimes allies of the FNLA, South Africa, or the United States. They were always an enemy of Neto and the MPLA. UNITA controls the bush in Angola.

ZAMISH
U.S. Military Assistance Mission in Zaire.

APPENDIX B

Chronology

Date	*Event*
30 Jun 60	Independence of the Democratic Republic of the Congo.
9 Jul 60	Katangan secession begins. Belgium intervenes as the ANC mutinies. Colonel Joseph Mobutu named ANC chief of staff. Katangan Gendarmerie recruited.
15 Jul 60–May 63	First UN troops arrive. United Nations campaigns for three years to restore the central government's control over the country.
29 May 63	Tshombe surrenders Katanga and goes into exile. The Katangan Gendarmerie crosses into Angola.
Apr 64–May 64	Minor uprisings in the eastern Congo expand into major rebellion due to the ANC's penchant for brutality and distaste for combat.
Jun 64	The Simba Rebellion explodes and consumes most of the eastern Congo. Tshombe returns from exile to become the prime minister.
5 Aug 64	Stanleyville, with over 1,500 expatriates, falls into rebel hands. Tshombe asks for help. Belgium dispatches Vandewalle to oversee the campaign against the Simbas. Mercenaries and the Katangan Gendarmerie return to fight under Tshombe's banner.
Mid-Sep 64	Vandewalle begins his campaign to retake the eastern Congo.
24 Nov 64	In Operation Dragon Rouge, the Belgian Paracommando Regiment, carried by American C-130s, retakes Stanleyville just ahead of Vandewalle's ground column, saving some 1,500 expatriates.
26 Nov 64	Operation Dragon Noir is conducted at Paulis. The Paracommando Regiment withdraws to Belgium.
Nov 64	War continues into the next year, and numerous expatriates are killed by the rebels in revenge.
29 Mar 65	Watsa falls to government forces, and the war is declared over.
25 Nov 65	General Mobutu seizes power. Tshombe goes into exile again.
1966	The Baka Regiment of the Katangan Gendarmerie mutinies in Stanleyville and is put down by Denard and mercenaries.
Jun 67	Tshombe is kidnapped and imprisoned in Algeria, where he dies two years later of a "heart attack."

Jul 67	Jean Schramme leads the mercenary revolt at Stanleyville, fights his way to Bukavu and holds that city for two months, and then crosses into Rwanda. Katangans fighting with him accept amnesty but are killed. Mobutu takes revenge against former gendarmes in Katanga province. Led by Mbumba, the Katangans return to exile in Angola.
1967–74	Mobutu consolidates power, ruins economy, and carries out his "authenticity" program.
Jul–Aug 75	Mobutu sends the FAZ against Neto's MPLA in Angola. The Cubans and the FNLC, formerly the Katangan Gendarmerie, rout the FAZ.
28 Feb 76	Mobutu and Neto sign the Brazzaville Accords, agreeing to end their support of opposition groups working against each other. Mobutu continues supporting UNITA.
8 Mar 77	The FNLC, led by Mbumba, crosses into Shaba in the first invasion, and the war lasts eighty days. The FAZ is still a disaster, and the Moroccans come to the rescue.
28 May 77	Mobutu claims victory over the FNLC. He purges the FAZ and conducts trials for ninety-one persons on various charges.
11 May 78	The FNLC crosses the Zambian border into Shaba, thus beginning Shaba II. The rebels move on Kolwezi.
13 May 78	The FNLC opens its attack on Kolwezi. The FAZ falls apart. The rebels capture the French military adviser team, and selected expatriates and locals are selected for trial.
	First word of the attack reaches the French Embassy. Gras sees Babia, and the 311th Airborne Battalion is placed on alert.
14 May 78	Executions of those found guilty of crimes against the "people" are under way in Kolwezi. The FNLC is still fairly disciplined. The FAZ still holds its headquarters in the new town.
	Gras pushes for French troops to encadre the FAZ's 311th and 133d Battalions. Mobutu asks for all kinds of help. The 311th and the 133d go to Lubumbashi to prepare for an overland drive on Kolwezi.
	Crisis cells operate in Brussels, Paris, and Washington.
15 May 78	Eight to ten expatriates are reported dead in Kolwezi. Morris-Knudsen prepares to evacuate its camp. Reports coming out via GECAMINES in Lubumbashi.
	The French Embassy is on 24-hour watch. Gras contacts the Belgian chargé to force a Belgian reaction to the situation. Mobutu calls in Major Mahele and gives him the order to drop one company on Kolwezi the next day.

16 May 78	At 0630, the 2d Company, 311th Airborne Battalion, begins its operation in Kolwezi and is destroyed. Its attack sets off the massacres in Kolwezi. The 311th's main body begins an overland march on Kolwezi. Morris-Knudsen delays its evacuations.

Gras sets up a planning staff and gets word of the 311th's operations. Combined planning begins with the Belgian military mission. Ambassador Ross calls for French intervention in cooperation with the Belgians and Americans.

President Carter places the 82d Airborne Division on alert and makes announcements to the press.

One company of the Belgian Paracommando Regiment and three C-130s are on alert under Operation Plan Samaritan. The alert is upgraded to the full regiment at midnight.

17 May 78 Sporadic slaughter continues in Kolwezi. Morris-Knudsen conducts its evacuation without problems.

The 311th reaches the Kolwezi airport by evening; it is cut off and out of ammunition.

Gras continues planning for an intervention and is notified that the 2d R.E.P. is on alert for Zaire. The tentative date of the operation is to be the 20th. French pilots are authorized to fly combat missions using FAZ Mirage fighters. Gras is placed in overall command of French forces.

At 0200, Colonel Depoorter receives orders to plan for a 72-hour operation in Kolwezi to evacuate the foreigners. The Paracommando Regiment prepares for deployment under Operation Red Bean. At 1900, the government gives a conditional "go" to the operation. Deployment is to begin the next day, with execution on the 20th. The Paracommandos are prohibited from coordinating with the French. The Belgian government discloses the Belgian and French movement alerts.

At 1030, the French 2d R.E.P. is alerted to be ready to move at 2000. Erulin has only a general idea of his mission.

18 May 78 Communications with Kolwezi are lost. Mobutu flies into the airport with news media to see Mahele.

Gras completes a plan and gets Paris' approval. Paris requests that the operation be moved up, and Gras refuses. Journiac makes the same request, and Gras refuses. Gras meets with Belgians and Americans to coordinate the operations. The Belgians are evasive, and when Gras is told the rebels have been ordered to kill their hostages and retreat, he moves the operation up to the 19th.

At 0220, Erulin is ordered to move the 2d R.E.P. to Solenarza Air Base for deployment to Zaire. The first aircraft departs at

1520. Erulin lands at Kinshasa at 2315 only to learn that the operation is to begin the next morning.

At 1315, the first C-130 of the Belgian 15th Wing takes off with Colonel Depoorter on board. Thirty-six hours later, the entire Paracommando Regiment is closed at Kamina.

19 May 78

The FNLC begins departing Kolwezi, leaving around 500 combatants behind along with local supporters. By now, most of the killing is over.

At 0330, the 2d R.E.P.'s briefing begins. The first assault wave is to go at dawn. Delays and equipment failures force the first wave to wait until 1050 for takeoff. The first wave is over Kolwezi at 1540.

The second wave is delayed further at Kamina. Gras cancels its drop until the 20th.

Erulin reports all objectives are secure before dark on the 19th. The 2d R.E.P. continues operations all night.

At 1400, the first Belgian aircraft lands at Kamina. Depoorter learns of the French operation and requests permission to conduct an assault landing before dark to reinforce the French. Brussels refuses but gives approval for the operation on the 20th. Depoorter redesigns his mission, and the unit prepares for action.

20 May 78

Erulin opens the day's operation with the 3d Company penetrating Manika. His second wave comes in at dawn to take the new town. A firefight breaks out between the 3d Company and the Paracommando Regiment.

Depoorter's first wave comes in on schedule at dawn. The 3d Para Battalion moves on the old town, followed shortly by the 1st Para Battalion. Lead units run into a firefight with the French.

Gras lands and grudgingly turns over the European quarters to the Belgians to evacuate the expatriates. The French continue to flush out the rebels. The French battle a large number of rebels at Metal-Shaba. By day's end, the Belgians have evacuated some 2,000 expatriates.

21 May 78

By sunset, Depoorter completes his mission and receives permission to withdraw to Kamina. Erulin continues operations. Vehicles arrive from Lubumbashi.

22 May 78

The Paracommando Regiment returns to Kamina and prepares for redeployment to Belgium. The 1st Para Battalion is detailed to stay behind until relieved by the 3d on 25 June. The 3d Para Battalion remains until July.

| 27 May 78 | The 2d R.E.P. moves to Lubumbashi, remains three weeks until the lead elements of the Inter-African Force arrive, and departs for Corsica. |

APPENDIX C

Organizational Charts of French and Belgian Units in Zaire

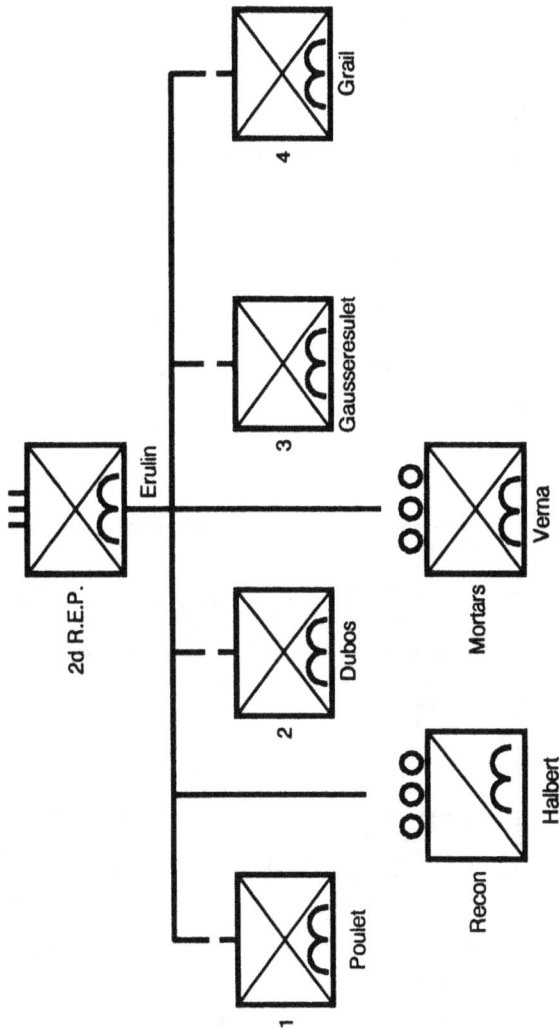

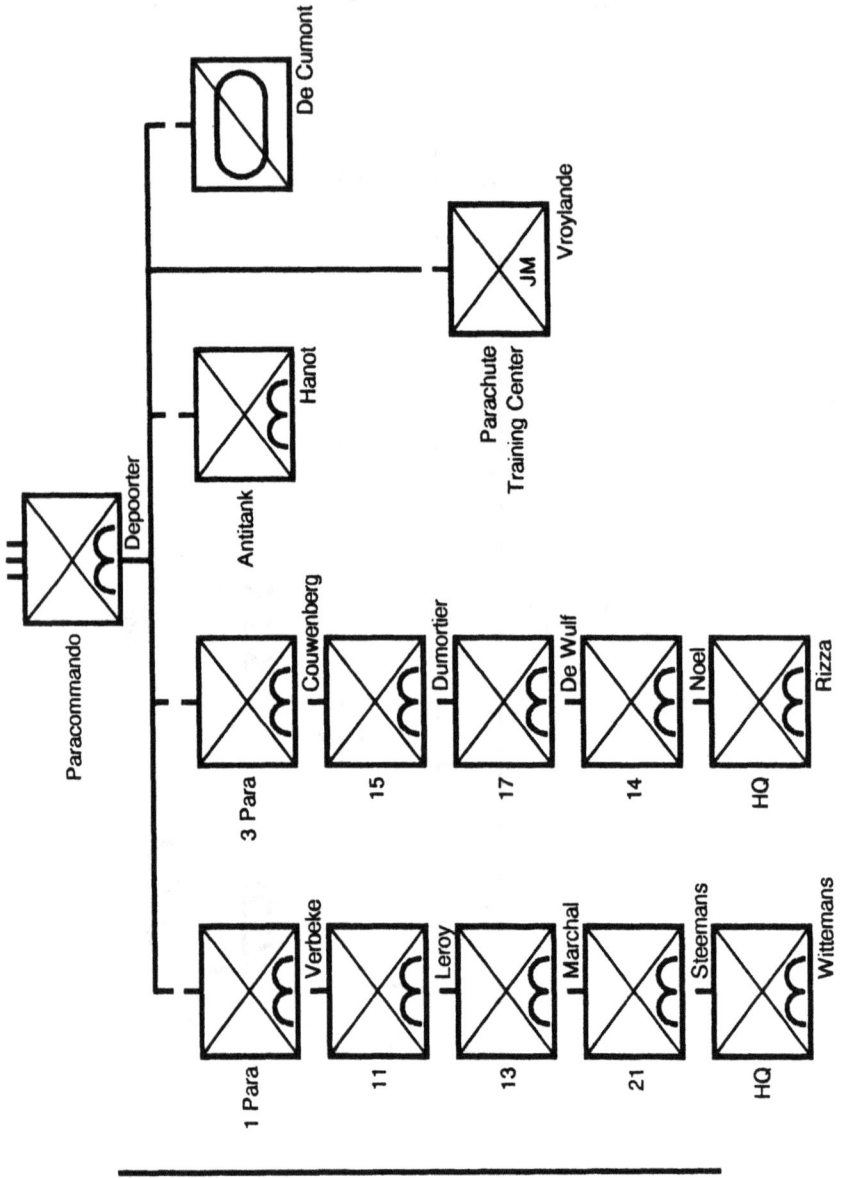

Paracommando — Depoorter

De Cumont

Antitank — Hanot

Parachute Training Center — Vroylande — JM

3 Para — Couwenberg
15 — Dumortier
17 — De Wulf
14 — Noel
HQ — Rizza

1 Para — Verbeke
11 — Leroy
13 — Marchal
21 — Steemans
HQ — Wittemans

NOTES

Chapter 2

1. Basil Davidson, *The Story of Africa* (London: Mitchell Beasley Publishers and Mitchell Beasley Television, 1984), 278; Tony Avirgan and Martha Honey, *War in Uganda: The Legacy of Idi Amin* (Westport, CT: Lawrence Hill & Co., 1982); and Joseph Conrad, *Heart of Darkness* and *The Secret Sharer* (New York: New American Library, 1983).

2. The number of volumes concerning this period in Zaire's history is enormous. As a sample, see Madeleine G. Kalb, *The Congo Cables: The Cold War in Africa—From Eisenhower to Kennedy* (New York: Macmillan Publishing Co., 1982); Ernest W. LeFever and Wynfred Joshua, *United Nations Peacekeeping in the Congo, 1960–1964: An Analysis of Political, Executive, and Military Control*, 4 vols. (Washington, DC: Brookings Institution, 1966); Edward Hymoff, *Stig Von Bayer: International Troubleshooter for Peace* (New York: James H. Heineman, 1965); A. G. Mezerik, ed., *Congo and the United Nations*, 3 vols. (New York: United Nations International Review Service, 1960–63); Conor Cruise O'Brien, *To Katanga and Back: A UN Case History* (New York: Simon & Schuster, 1962); Frédéric J. L. A. Vandewalle, *L'Ommengang: Odyssée et Reconquête de Stanleyville, 1964* (Brussels: Le Livre Africain, Collection Temoinage Africain, 1970); Merwin Crawford Young, *Politics in the Congo: Decolonization and Independence* (Princeton, NJ: Princeton University Press, 1965); Merwin Crawford Young and Thomas Turner, *The Rise and Decline of the Zairian State* (Madison: University of Wisconsin Press, 1985); and Stephen R. Weissman, *American Foreign Policy in the Congo, 1960–1964* (Ithaca, NY: Cornell University, 1965).

3. Young and Turner, 255; and Peter Mangold, "Shaba I and Shaba II," *Survival* 21 (May–June 1979):109.

4. See Vandewalle; Fred E. Wagoner, *Dragon Rouge: The Rescue of Hostages in the Congo* (Washington, DC: National Defense University, 1980); David Reed, *111 Days in Stanleyville* (New York: Harper & Row, 1965); Mike Hoare, *Congo Mercenary* (London: Robert Hale & Co., 1967); Lois Carlson, *Monganga Paul* (New York: Harper & Row, 1966); Jo Wasson Hoyt, *For the Love of Mike* (New York: Random House, 1966); Howard M. Epstein, ed., *Revolt in the Congo, 1960–1964* (New York: Facts on File, 1965); William Attwood, *The Reds and the Blacks: A Personal Adventure* (New York: Harper & Row, 1967); Gerry S. Thomas, *Mercenary Troops in Modern Africa* (Boulder, CO: Westview Press, 1984); Homer E. Dowdy, *Out of the Jaws of the Lion* (New York: Harper & Row, 1965); and Thomas P. Odom, *Dragon Operations: Hostage Rescues in the Congo, 1964–1965*, Leavenworth Papers no. 14 (Fort Leavenworth, KS: Combat Studies Institute, U.S. Army Command and General Staff College, 1988).

5. See Wagoner; Reed; Vandewalle; Hoare; Dowdy; and Odom.

6. Young and Turner, 50–54.

7. Kalb, 89–101.

8. Ibid., 4–7, 23–24, 175–77.

9. Young and Turner, 52, 57–58.

10. Ibid., 250–51; and Irving Kaplan, ed., *Zaire: A Country Study* (Washington, DC: American University, 1979), 259–60.

11. Young and Turner, 57–58, 251, 419. These authors report that Tshombe's kidnapping was beyond the capability of the Congolese security services as it required a support network that spanned from Africa to Europe. Though accusations have ranged from the CIA to the KGB, the perpetrators remain unknown. The same cloud of mystery hangs over the report of Tshombe's "heart attack"; that seems fitting considering Tshombe's probable involvement in the equally mysterious death of Patrice Lumumba. Schramme had been involved in the Katanga secession and formed his own unit, the Bataillon Leopard. Following Tshombe's surrender, Schramme crossed into Angola with 7 mercenaries and 500 Katangans. He and his unit returned at Tshombe's call in 1964 and fought in the war against the Simbas. Schramme later published *Le Bataillon Léopard* as an account of his exploits. The book is interesting reading but of doubtful value as history.

12. Young and Turner, 251–53.

13. Ibid.

14. Ibid., 255.

15. Kaplan, 218–20.

16. Kalb, 379–80; and Kaplan, 100–101.

17. Kalb, 379–81.

18. F. S. B. Kazadi, "Mobutu, MPR, and the Politics of Survival," *Africa Report* (January-February 1978):11; and Kaplan, 62–65.

19. Kaplan, 65–66, 99–101, 260–61; Kalb, 381–82; and Young and Turner, 372–73.

20. Ibid.

21. Young and Turner, 253–54, 376–78, 448, 464.

22. Ibid., 448.

23. Ibid., 376–78. Young and Turner point out that Mobutu was gambling on a broad scale. He was anti-MPLA because of its Communist backing, not only from the Soviets and the Cubans but from the Brazzaville government as well. An MPLA victory in Angola would put Communist countries on Zaire's north and south. Mobutu had territorial ambitions on the Cabinda enclave and had been supporting the rebel Front for the Liberation of the Cabinda Enclave also. Finally, if he could pull off the gamble, he would have established himself as the African leader of the day.

24. Ibid.

25. Ibid., 254.

26. Ibid.

27. Ibid.; Colin Legum, "Zaire," in *Africa Contemporary Record: Annual Survey and Documents 1976-1977*, vol. 9 (New York: Africana Publishing Co., 1977), B534–35 (hereafter referred to as *ACR 76–77*. For a firsthand account of the CIA operation to funnel money and supplies to support this war, see John Stockwell, *In Search of*

Enemies: A CIA Story (New York: W. W. Norton, 1978). For a firsthand account of two mercenaries involved with the operation, see Chris Dempster and Dave Tomkins, *Fire Power* (New York: St. Martin's Press, 1980).

Chapter 3

1. Kenneth L. Adelman, "Old Foes and New Friends," *Africa Report* (January-February 1978):5; Legum, *ACR 76–77*, B527–28; and Malutama di Malu, "The Shaba Invasions" (Fort Leavenworth, KS: U.S. Army Command and General Staff College, 1981), 26–30.

2. Malu, 31–32.

3. Ibid., 33; and Pierre Sergent, *La Légion Saute Sur Kolwezi* (Paris: Presses de la Cité, 1978), 34–35.

4. Malu, 33–34.

5. Ibid., 35–36.

6. Ibid., 37–38.

7. Adelman, 5–6; and Gerald J. Bender, "Angola, the Cubans, and American Anxieties," *Foreign Policy* 31 (Summer 1978):15.

8. Adelman, 6.

9. Colin Legum, "Zaire," in *Africa Contemporary Record: Annual Survey and Documents, 1978–1979*, vol. 11 (New York: Africana Publishing Co., 1980), B572 (hereafter referred to as *ACR 78–79*).

10. Mangold, 109; Adelman, 6–7; and Oye Ogunbadejo, "Conflict in Africa: A Case Study of the Shaba Crisis, 1977," *World Affairs* 141 (Winter 1979):229.

11. Adelman, 7.

12. Ibid.; and Thomas A. Marks, "The Shaba Adventure," *Africa Institute Bulletin* 16 (No. 3, 1978).

13. Adelman, 8; Kaplan, 99; and Ogunbadejo, 226.

14. Adelman, 8; Mangold, 109; and Kaplan, 99–101.

15 Adelman, 8; and Ogunbadejo, 226–27.

16. Ibid.; and General Yves Gras, "L'opération Kolwezi," *Mondes et Cultures* 45 (8 November 1985):693.

17. Sergent, 67–68.

18. Ibid., 26–27; and Gras, 693.

19. Young and Turner, 374–75; Mangold, 110; and Adelman, 8–9.

20. Ogunbadejo, 226–27; and Mangold, 110.

21. Adelman, 8–9; Young and Turner, 374–75; and Mangold, 110.

22. Malu, 38–54.

116

23. Young and Turner, 257; and Malu, 72. In Mangold, on page 110, the number of refugees is reported at 50,000 to 70,000.

24. Malu, 72–73; and Kaplan, 67–69.

25. Kaplan, 75; and Gras, 693.

26. Mangold, 110–11; Adelman, 10; and Legum, *ACR 78–79*, B571–72.

27. Kazadi, 11–12; and Adelman, 9.

28. Adelman, 9–10; Legum, *ACR 78–79*, B572; and Kaplan, 101.

29. Mangold, 108; Legum, *ACR 78–79*, B573; and Adelman, 10.

Chapter 4

1. Accounts on the number of FNLC members involved in the invasion range from a high of 5,000 to a more conservative 2,000. The same holds true on their route; it is not clear if all the force came through Zambia or only a group headed toward Kolwezi. While of interest, the critical issue was that the Kolwezi assault group did use Zambia and remained undetected. See Malu, 55; "Massacre in Zaire," *U.S. News & World Report* (5 June 1978):41; Kyenga Sana, "Kolwezi Liberated," *Brussels Special* (29 May 1978):10–12 (translated in *JPRS*); Rudolf Schmidt, "Zaire After the 1978 Shaba Crisis," *Aussen Politik*, English edition, 30 (1st Quarter 1979):88; Legum, *ACR 78–79*, B574; and Message, AMEMBASSY Lusaka to SECSTATE WASHDC, 01738, DTG 151203Z May 78, Shaba Incursions: Use of Zambian Territory.

2. Colin Legum, "Zaire," in *Africa Contemporary Record: Annual Survey and Documents, 1977–1978*, vol. 10 (New York: Africana Publishing Co., 1979), B574 (hereafter referred to as *ACR 77–78*); Paul Emmanuel, "Disorganization, Corruption in Kolwezi," *Brussels Special* (21 June 1978) (translated in *JPRS*); and Sergent, 17–18.

3. Colonel Phillipe Erulin, "Kolwezi," unpublished script to a presentation at the U.S. Army War College, Carlisle Barracks, PA, date unknown; Raymond Carroll, James Pringle, and James O. Goldsborough, "Massacre in Zaire," *Newsweek* (29 May 1978):39; Schmidt, 92; Mangold, 111; and Sergent, 36–37.

4. Legum, *ACR 77–78*, B574; Sergent, 36–37; Message, SECSTATE WASHDC to AMEMBASSY Kinshasa, 123864, 160120Z May 78, Situation in Shaba as of 1500 (EDT) May 15, 1978; Schmidt, 88; and Emmanuel.

5. Sergent, 19–22.

6. Ibid., 22–23.

7. Ibid., 22–23, 229; Colonel Yves Gras, Chef, Mission Militaire Francaise au Zaire, "Journal de Marche du 13 Mai au 15 Juin 1978" (hereafter cited as MMF).

8. Legum, *ACR 77–78*, B574–75; Sergent, 53; "Massacre in Zaire"; and Erulin.

9. Carroll, et al., 35; and Sergent, 28–29.

10. I have related the narrative from the French perspective for two reasons: first, there are more sources available on the French, and second, the French are the dominant actors in this episode. Sergent, 28–29; and Gras, 693.

11. Sergent, 29, 33–35.

12. MMF; and Sergent, 30. Sergent reports that it was Gras who saw Babia rather than Larzul. I relied on the MMF journal as the official record. This is a minor point, but Sergent goes to great lengths to emphasize Gras' role.

13. Sergent, 30–31.

14. Ibid., 32, 35–36; and MMF.

15. Sergent, 31–33; Legum, *ACR 77–78*, B575; Carroll, et al., 35; and Emmanuel, 58. Emmanuel reported that the failure to warn authorities in Kolwezi was due to pure bureaucratic incompetence.

16. Sergent, 36–37; MMF; and Gras, 693. Again, Sergent reports that Gras went to see Babia when the MMF journal indicates Larzul was also present.

17. Sergent, 37. In examining State Department records on Shaba II, I could not find a single message tagged for the crisis before 15 May. As for the American news media, the crisis did not make the newspapers before the 15th either. In the case of the Belgians, the situation was headline news on the 14th. Unfortunately, I did not have access to the Belgian message traffic. However, it appears that both the United States and Belgium waited until the 15th to form crisis teams. While I have no information on whether Belgian Prime Minister Tindemans or Foreign Minister Simonet telephoned Mobutu on the 13th, I feel secure in saying that President Carter or even Secretary Vance probably did not. President d'Estaing's call to Mobutu is just another example of his focus on Africa. Message, SECSTATE WASHDC to AMEMBASSY Kinshasa, 122789, DTG 150239Z May 78, Shaba Incursions: Interagency Task Force; and Henri J. G. Depoorter, "Kolwezi," *Military Review* (September 1979):32.

18. Sergent, 49–51.

19. Ibid., 49–58.

20. Ibid., 43–44.

21. Ibid., 44–45.

22. Ibid., 45–46; Gras, 694; and MMF.

23. Sergent, 46; Gras, 694; and MMF.

24. Sergent, 46–47.

25. Gras, 693–94; and MMF.

26. Ibid.; and Sergent, 47–48. It is impossible to establish the exact sequence of meetings on the 14th, and I have used my own judgment in depicting them. While I am not absolutely sure they occurred in the order shown, I am convinced that they did occur.

27. Message, SECSTATE WASHDC, 122789; Depoorter, 32; Legum, *ACR 77–78*, B577; Message, AMEMBASSY Kinshasa to SECSTATE WASHDC, 04793, DTG 151507Z May 78, Shaba Attack: Expedited FMS Deliveries; Message, AMEMBASSY Kinshasa to SECSTATE WASHDC, 04785, DTG 151343Z May 78, Shaba Attack: W/W AMCITS at Kolwezi; Message, AMEMBASSY Kinshasa to SECSTATE WASHDC, 04808, 151946Z May 78, W/W US Citizens in Zaire; President Jimmy

Carter, Presidential Determination No. 78-11, Memorandum for the Secretary of State, Subject: Assistance to Zaire, 18 May 1978.

28. "Mobutu demande l'aide étrangère pour faire face à l'invasion du Shaba," *Le Soir* (14 May 1978):1, 3; and "Sommaire: Kolwezi 78," *Forum de la Force Terrestre* (September-October 1978):6.

29. Sergent, 63–64; MMF; and Gras, 694–95.

30. Gras, 695; Sergent, 64–65; and MMF.

31. Gras, 695; MMF; and Sergent, 69–72.

32. Sergent, 80–81. A darker interpretation of Mobutu's decision to use the 311th was that he intended to force the West to intervene in order to save its citizens. As a military man, Mobutu must have known the risks involved. Such an interpretation assumes that he saw the dangers and deliberately chose to sacrifice the 311th as a means of stimulating a Western response.

33. Ibid.

Chapter 5

1. Sergent, 82–83; MMF; and Gras, 695. The original plan had been to drop the 2d Company from two C-130s. But when one aircraft developed engine problems, Colonel Yeka ordered the drop to go in two waves of sixty troops each. It was truly an incredibly stupid operation from its conception to its ill-fated end. Message, AMEMBASSY Kinshasa to SECSTATE WASHDC, 04934, DTG 171947Z May 78, Shaba Invasion-SITREP 3 (May 17, 1978).

2. Sergent, 84. Sergent makes some conclusions on this that do not make sense. First, he says that the FAZ troops thought the drop was a Cuban operation, and then, he says this caused the FAZ to collapse. But other sources speak of the 2d Company survivors making it to the FAZ headquarters. I believe the survivors of the airborne operation probably demoralized the FAZ headquarters that had been waiting for relief for three days only to see it wiped out.

3. Ibid., 85–86. Again, Sergent's logic is faulty as to the origin of the slaughter on the 16th. He implies that it was caused by a report by the FNLC on the airborne operation to their liaison in Brussels. He says that these FNLC politicians changed the wording to reflect a European airborne operation and issued a press release claiming to have killed 100 European paratroops. Then, Western news agencies picked up the reports and broadcast them as fact. The FNLC, on hearing the reports, blamed the Europeans and started killing them.

All of this is apparently true, but the reports did not get out until the 17th, and Sergent reports the massacres began on the 16th. He further claims that the Cuban advisers to the FNLC departed after the drop, and this loss of control allowed the FNLC's discipline to fail.

I do not support either claim. It appears that the FNLC was already apprehensive and upset when the 2d Company jumped. The rebels probably turned on the expatriates out of fear and resentment. They probably believed a major counterattack was in progress and began killing the Europeans in response.

Legum has difficulty explaining the killings. First, he accuses the FAZ of using the expatriates as hostages against rebel attacks. On the other hand, he also suggests, based on refugee reports, that the French training mission that jumped with the 2d Company started the killings. The reports of the survivors of the massacre do not support the first claim, and the MMF journal and Gras document that the 311th went to Lubumbashi without its advisers. Legum, *ACR 77–78*, B574–75.

4. Sergent, 88–90.

5. Ibid., 91; Gras, 695–96; MMF; and Malu, 58–59. Once again, I have to break with Sergent's account. Out of all the sources, he is the only one who states that Major Mahele made it to Kolwezi on the 16th. He also states that Mobutu flew into the airfield on the 17th. All sources say that Mobutu made a news media event of the trip on the 18th. Had Mahele taken the airfield on the 16th, I do not believe Mobutu would have waited until the 18th.

6. Gras, 695–96; MMF; and Message, SECSTATE WASHDC to AMEMBASSY Paris, 123886, DTG 160836Z May 78, Discussion With French and Belgians on Shaba.

7. Gras, 695–96; MMF; and Sergent, 75–76, 80–81. If Mobutu had staged the 311th's operation in order to stimulate a Western intervention, I believe he would have notified the Western officials at this interview. Instead, he waited until the news of the operation came in, and he still maintained that it had been a success.

8. Sergent, 76–77; Message, SECSTATE WASHDC Info AMEMBASSY Monrovia, 123870, DTG 160125Z May 78, Shaba Invasion SITREP 1 (May 15, 1978). According to this message, the rebels had tried to consolidate the expatriates on the 13th but had given up after learning that there were 3,000 in Kolwezi. According to Sergent, Ross' cable resulted in another phone call by d'Estaing to Mobutu, who repeated his earlier assertion that all was going well.

9. Sergent, 77–78.

10. Ibid., 79; Gras, 695–96; and MMF.

11. Message, AMEMBASSY Kinshasa to AMCONSUL Lubumbashi, 04811, DTG 160110Z May 78, Shaba Invasion: Evacuation of CIS Personnel From Kolwezi; Message, SECSTATE WASHDC to AMEMBASSY Kinshasa, 123864; Message, SECSTATE WASHDC to AMEMBASSY Kinshasa, 124005, DTG 161610Z May 78, Shaba SITREP NO. 3 as of 1000 Hours GMT, May 16; Message AMEMBASSY Kinshasa to SECSTATE WASHDC, 04863, DTG 161733Z May 78, Shaba Attack: Evacuation of CIS Personnel From Kolwezi; Message, AMEMBASSY Kinshasa to SECSTATE WASHDC, 04865, 161753Z May 78, Shaba Attack: Conversation With Mobutu; Message, AMEMBASSY Paris to SECSTATE WASHDC, 15476, DTG 161737Z May 78, Discussions With French on Shaba; Message, SECSTATE WASHDC to AMEMBASSY Paris, 123886, DTG 160836Z May 78, Discussion With French and Belgians on Shaba; Message, AMEMBASSY Kinshasa to SECSTATE WASHDC, 04841, DTG 161257Z May 78, Shaba Invasion (SITREP2)—May 16, 1978; Message, SECSTATE WASHDC to AMEMBASSY Kinshasa, 125209, DTG 171230Z May 78, Shaba SITREP NO. 4: 2300 GMT May 16; Message, AMEMBASSY Kinshasa to SECSTATE WASHDC, 04844, DTG 161413Z May 78, Consolate Lubumbashi Input to Shaba Invasion SITREP 2; Message, AMEMBASSY Kinshasa to SECSTATE WASHDC, 04880, DTG 170027Z May 78,

Shaba Attack: Evacuation of CIS Personnel From Kolwezi; "U.S. Set to Evacuate 73 Citizens in Zaire," *The New York Times* (17 May 1978):A1, A8; and Message, SECSTATE WASHDC to AMEMBASSY Paris 125187, DTG 170307Z May 78, Shaba Incursion: Possible Rescue Effort.

12. Odom, 54.

13. Ibid.; and Depoorter, 30–31.

14. "Sommaire: Kolwezi 78," 12–13; and Emile Genot, *Bérets rouges, Bérets verts . . . 50,000 Paracommandos* (Brussels: Gutenberg Editions, 1986), 266.

15. Depoorter, 32; Genot, 264–65; "Sommaire: Kolwezi 78," 6–7; and Message, AMEMBASSY Brussels to SECSTATE WASHDC, 09311, DTG 161816Z May 78, Shaba Incursions: Belgian Reaction.

16. Ibid.

17. Sergent, 91–95; Malu, 58–59; MMF; and Gras, 696. It appears that the company of the 133d was at the bridge to protect it as originally planned by Gras. However, Gras and Mahele did not know that it was there. Malu reports that Mahele took the company with him to Kolwezi as does the MMF journal and Gras. Sergent reports that Mahele told the company commander to hold or die.

18. Ibid.

19. Carroll, et al., 35; Sergent, 89; "Massacre in Zaire," 41–42; Message, AMEMBASSY Kinshasa to SECSTATE WASHDC, 04946, DTG 181113Z May 78, Shaba II SITREP, 18 May 1978; Message, AMEMBASSY Kinshasa to SECSTATE WASHDC, 04943, DTG 180955Z May 78, Shaba Attack—SITREP 4 (May 18, 1978); Message, AMEMBASSY Kinshasa to SECSTATE WASHDC, 04919, DTG 171500Z May 78, Shaba Attack: Status Report on CIS Evacuation of Kolwezi Base Camp: 1230 ZULU May 17; Paul Emmanuel, "We Will Return to Kolwezi," *Brussels Special* (14 June 1978):50–53 (translated in *JPRS*).

20. Message, AMEMBASSY Kinshasa to SECSTATE WASHDC, 04880; Message, SECSTATE WASHDC to AMEMBASSY Paris, 125187; Message, AMEMBASSY Kinshasa to SECSTATE WASHDC, 04882, DTG 170817Z May 78, Status Report on CIS Evacuation of Kolwezi Base Camp; Message, AMEMBASSY Kinshasa to SECSTATE WASHDC, 04899, DTG 171028Z May 78, Status Report CIS Evacuation of Kolwezi Base Camp as of 0939 ZULU; Message, AMEMBASSY Kinshasa to SECSTATE WASHDC, 04902, DTG 171129Z May 78; Shaba Attack: Status Report of CIS Evacuation of Kolwezi Camp, 1030 ZULU; Message, AMCONSUL Lubumbashi to AMEMBASSY Kinshasa, 00489, DTG 171305Z May 78, E and E Plan; Message, AMEMBASSY Kinshasa to SECSTATE WASHDC, 04919; Message, SECSTATE WASHDC to AMEMBASSY Kinshasa, 125218, DTG 171415Z May 78, Shaba SITREP No. 5 as of 1000 GMT, May 17; Message, AMEMBASSY Kinshasa to SECSTATE WASHDC 04921, DTG 171527Z May 78, Shaba Attack: Status Report on CIS Evacuation of Kolwezi Base Camp, 1430 ZULU.

21. Sergent, 107–8.

22. MMF.

23. Message, AMCONSUL Lubumbashi to SECSTATE WASHDC, 00482, 171044Z May 78, Shaba Attack: Why Kolwezi?

24. Gras, 697; and Sergent, 110–11.

25. Ibid.; and MMF.

26. Sergent, 101–2; Colonel Phillipe Erulin, Commandant le 2éme Régiment Étranger de Parachutistes, a Monsieur le Général, Commandant la 11éme Division Parachutiste, "Objét: Opération Bonité," Calvi, France, 24 June 1978; Colonel Phillipe Erulin, "Mission Accomplie: Entretien avec le colonel Erulin, commandant le 2éme R.E.P.," *Armées Aujourdhui* (July-August 1978):14; and Colonel Phillipe Erulin, *Zaire, Sauver Kolwezi: Un reportage photographique* (Paris: Eric Baschet Éditions, 1979), 1.

27. Pierre Vandervoorde, *Paras du Monde Entier* (Namur, Belgium: Wesmael-Charlier, 1981), 221–23.

28. Erulin, "Objet: Opération Bonité"; Erulin, "Mission Accomplie," 14; and Sergent, 102, 240.

29. Sergent, 101, 104–6; Erulin, "Objet: Opération Bonité"; and Lieutenant Colonel Jacques Hatte, "Kolwezi: An Airborne Assault," *Infantry* (May 1979):25.

30. Gras, 696–97; and Sergent, 111.

31. The Belgian government came under fire from the Belgian press over its handling of the crisis. Mobutu also took advantage of the situation to blast Brussels for its slow response while at the same time he asked for more aid. The Belgian public apparently approved the action finally taken but was equally sure that the response had come too late. Despite Simonet's statement on it only being a difference in perspective, he later referred to the French action as a form of colonialism. At the same time, however, he admitted the 2d R.E.P. had been decisive in saving lives. Prime Minister Tindemans made the link with 1964 when he said the deployment of the paras could have started new massacres. Jacques Cordy, "Voler au secours de Mobutu? La France hésite. . . ," *Le Soir* (17 May 1978):page number unknown; J.v.C., "L'intervention belge à Stanleyville en novembre 1964," *Le Soir* (17 May 1978):page number unknown; Robert Falony, "La plus grande prudence," *Le Peuple* (17 May 1978):1; Susa Nudelhole, "Gendarmes," *le drapeau rouge* (17 May 1978):1; "Inquiétude sur le sort des Européens a Kolwezi," *La Libre Belgique* (17 May 1978):1, 4; "S'il faut sauver les Européens bloqués à Kolwezi, les mesures nécessaire ont été prises," *Le Soir* (18 May 1978):1, 3; "Préoccupation no. 1: l'évacuation éventuelle des Occidentaux de Kolwezi," *Le Soir* (18 May 1978):3; "M. Henri Simonet à la Chambre: il ne s'agirait pas d'une immixtion," *Le Soir* (18 May 1978):3; Jacques Cordy, "La France n'entend pas se faire 'pieger' au Zaire, mais se la 'guerre' du Shaba devait s'aggraver. . . ," *Le Soir* (18 May 1978):3; Jean-Paul Vankeerbergen, "La canonnière," *La drapeau rouge* (18 May 1978); Alain de Fooz, "Are We Prepared?" *Brussels Special* (12 June 1978):10–12 (translated in *JPRS*); "Belgian Public Opinion Poll Approves Shaba Intervention, *Brussels Special* (14 June 1978):8–9 (translated in *JPRS*); "Commentary on Shaba Military Intervention," *La Libre Belgique* (24 May 1978) (translated in *JPRS*); "Des paras belges et francais sont partis, mais une solution pacifique reste possible," *Le Soir* (19 May 1978):1–3; "Paras belges et francais au Zaire; Pour la France le sauvetage concernerait aussi les Zairois," *Le Soir* (19 May 1978):3; Frédéric Kiesel, "Des soucis ambigus," *La Cité* (18 May 1978):1; "L'opération de sauvetage des Européens de Kolwezi sera-t-elle nécessaire?" *La Libre Belgique* (19 May 1978):1; "Le Fil des Événements, Rue de la Loi," *La Libre Belgique* (19 May 1978):page number unknown; "Irritation zairoise contre M. Simonet," *La Libre Belgique* (19 May

1978):page number unknown; D. de M., "Paris: le gouvernement veut garder son sang-froid," *La Libre Belgique* (19 May 1978):3; "Les Européens de Kolwezi pris dans les combats et poursuivis par la haine des ex-gendarmes," *La Libre Belgique* (19 May 1978):page number unknown; "La situation au Shaba prime toutes les autres préoccupations gouvernementales," *Le Peuple* (19 May 1978):1; "Shaba: C'est L'aventure Neo-Coloniale," *Le drapeau rouge* (19 May 1978):1; and "Paras belges et francais ont commencé une opération de sauvetage," *La Dernière Heure* (19 May 1978):28.

32. Legum, *ACR 77-78*, B576; Message, AMEMBASSY Paris to SECSTATE WASHDC, 15662, DTG 171734Z May 78, Shaba Incursion: Possible Rescue Effort; Message, AMEMBASSY Kinshasa to SECSTATE WASHDC, 04935, DTG 172004Z May 78, Shaba Attack: Zairian Government Request for U.S. Assistance in International Contingency Operation; Message, SECSTATE WASHDC to AMEMBASSY Kinshasa, 126030, DTG 180138Z May 78, Situation in Shaba as of 2000 Hours (GMT), May 17, 1978 (No. 6); Message, SECSTATE WASHDC to AMEMBASSY Kinshasa-Flash 126065, DTG 180609Z May 78, Shaba Incursion Zairian Government Request for U.S. Assistance in International Contingency Operation; Message, SECSTATE WASHDC to AMEMBASSY Kinshasa, Flash 126070, DTG 180743Z May 78, Shaba Incursion Zairian Government Request for U.S. Assistance in International Contingency Operation; "Most Americans Said to Leave War Zone," *The New York Times* (18 May 1978):A3.

Chapter 6

1. Sergent, 117–18; Gras, 698; and MMF.

2. Sergent, 128–29; Gras, 698; and MMF.

3. Gras, 699; MMF; and Emmanuel, "Disorganization, Corruption in Kolwezi."

4. MMF.

5. Gras, 699. Gras says that the Belgians' decision to fly into Kamina made a cooperative venture impossible. Message, AMEMBASSY Kinshasa to SECSTATE WASHDC, 04993, DTG 182127Z May 78, Shaba Attack: Airborne Operations Planning; and MMF.

6. Gras, 699; MMF; and Sergent, 130–31.

7. Sergent, 121–23; Erulin, "Objet: Opération Bonité"; Erulin, "Mission Accomplie," 14–15; and Hatte, 25.

8. Sergent, 122–26; Erulin, "Objet: Opération Bonité"; Erulin, "Mission Accomplie," 14–15; and Hatte, 25.

9. Erulin, "Objet: Opération Bonité"; Sergent, 135–36; and Erulin, "Kolwezi."

10. Ibid.

11. Sergent, 137–38.

12. Ibid.

13. Ibid., 139–40; and Gras, 700.

14. "Ordre Initial D'opération Concernant L'engagement du 2éme R.E.P. à Kolwezi Par O.A.P. le 19 Mai 78," Kinshasa, Zaire, 19 May 1978 (0400A); and Gras, 700.

15. "Ordre Initial D' opération . . . ."

16. Ibid.

17. Ibid.

18. Ibid.

19. Ibid.; and Erulin, "Kolwezi."

20. Sergent, 118–19.

21. Ibid., 140–44; Gras, 700; MMF; and Erulin, "Objet: Opération Bonité."

22. Sergent, 142–46; Gras, 700; MMF; and Erulin, "Objet: Opération Bonité."

23. Sergent, 148–50; Hatte, 26–27; and Paul Fanshaw, "Target Kolwezi," *Soldier of Fortune* (December 1983):51–52.

24. Sergent, 152–53; Fanshaw, 52; Hatte, 27; Erulin, "Objet: Opération Bonité"; and Erulin, "Kolwezi."

25. Sergent, 155–57.

26. Ibid., 157–58; Fanshaw, 52–54; and MMF.

27. Sergent, 159–60.

28. Ibid.

29. Ibid., 160–61.

30. "Ordre Initial D' opération . . ."; and Legum, *ACR 77–78*, B576.

31. Sergent, 163–64.

32. Ibid., 164–68.

33. Ibid., 169–72.

34. Ibid., 173–77.

35. Ibid.; Gras, 701; Erulin, "Objet: Opération Bonité"; and MMF.

36. Sergent, 169, 181–82; and Erulin, "Objet: Opération Bonité."

37. Sergent, 182–84; and Erulin, "Objet Opération Bonité."

38. Ibid.

39. Ibid.

Chapter 7

1. Depoorter, 32; Genot, 264–66; and "Sommaire: Kolwezi 78," 7.

2. Depoorter, 32; Genot, 264–66, 284; "Sommaire: Kolwezi 78," 5–7, 12–13.

3. Major Henrot, "Des vérités bonnes à dire," *Monde* (month unknown, 1978):48–51. Major Henrot, serving in Red Bean as a liaison officer, was the last Belgian officer

on the ground in the withdrawal from Paulis. Genot, 284; Odom, 140–44; and "Sommaire: Kolwezi 78," 24.

4. Genot, 266; "Sommaire: Kolwezi 78," 7–8; and Depoorter, 32.

5. Mr. Vanden Boeynants later defended the disclosure as being necessary to let the rebels know that the Paracommandos were coming to conduct an evacuation and thereby to avoid possible misunderstandings. "Commentary on Shaba Military Intervention"; Depoorter, 32; Lieutenant Colonel BEM P. Malherbe, Letter to Colonel Depoorter Concerning Kolwezi, March 1981.

6. Depoorter, 32; Genot, 266–67; and "Sommaire: Kolwezi 78," 7–10, 12.

7. "Sommaire: Kolwezi 78," 10–11; and Genot, 266–67.

8. Ibid.

9. Genot, 268–69; "Sommaire: Kolwezi 78," 11–12; and Depoorter, 32–33.

10. Depoorter, 32–33; "Sommaire: Kolwezi 78," 11–13; Genot, 268–69; Major BEM P. Malherbe, "Nous sommes fiers de nos hommes et de notre operation," UN Officer Supérieur Belge Témoigne sur Kolwezi: Nous sommes fiers de nos hommes et de notre opération," newspaper article from unknown Belgian paper, date unknown; Malherbe, Letter to General Depoorter; and Henrot, 50.

11. "Sommaire: Kolwezi 78," 13; and Genot, 270.

12. Ibid.; and Depoorter, 33.

13. "Sommaire: Kolwezi 78," 13.

14. Sergent, 187.

15. Ibid., 187–88.

16. Ibid., 188.

17. Ibid., 189.

18. "Sommaire: Kolwezi 78," 14; Genot, 272; and Depoorter, 33.

19. "Sommaire: Kolwezi 78," 15–16; Genot, 272; and Depoorter, 33.

20. Sergent, 185–86; and Hatte, 28–29.

21. Sergent, 185–86. The Belgians claim that their units, rather than French units, discovered the slaughterhouse. I do not doubt that the Belgians found the site, but I believe that it was well after the French had found it. The Belgians make no mention of any survivors, a fact that indicates the French had been there ahead of them. In addition, the Belgians report that the unit that found the massacre was attached to the 1st Para Battalion, which had not moved off toward the new town until well after the 4th Company, 2d R.E.P., had jumped. "Sommaire: Kolwezi 78," 17; and Genot, 275. Genot mentions a "Mr. Radu" and describes how this individual, though wounded, had hidden under the bodies and then in a toilet. It seems this is a summary of the experiences of Ms. Radu, Mr. Jurmann, and Mr. Michel.

22. MMF; Genot, 272; "Sommaire: Kolwezi 78," 16; Sergent, 192; and Gras, 701.

23. Sergent, 189–90; and Genot, 284.

24. Sergent claims that the Belgians opened fire on the 3d Company. Erulin mentioned it in his after-action report, but he did not make any specific accusations. Major Couwenberg, the 3d Para Battalion commander, claims the French fired on his lead units, a claim supported by Depoorter, Malherbe, and Genot. Colonel Malherbe told me that the French were attempting to intimidate the Paracommando Regiment into stopping the evacuation. I believe it was more likely to have been a natural result of attempting to conduct the operations independently. Sergent, 190–91; Erulin, "Objet: Opération Bonité"; Genot, 273; A. Couwenberg, "Belgians at Kolwezi—Infantry Letters," *Infantry* (July-August 1980):55; and Colonel BEM P. Malherbe, commander, Belgian Paracommando Regiment, Interview with author, Everberg, Belgium, 24 November 1988.

25. MMF; Sergent, 192; Gras, 701; Genot, 272–73; Depoorter, 34; and "Sommaire: Kolwezi 78," 17.

26. MMF; Sergent, 192–93; Gras, 701–702; Genot, 273–76; Depoorter, 34; and Erulin, "Objet: Opération Bonité."

27. Sergent, 191–92, 203; MMF; and Gras, 702.

28. Ibid.

29. Sergent, 203–6.

30. MMF; and "Sommaire: Kolwezi 78," 17–18.

31. "Sommaire: Kolwezi 78," 17–18; and Carroll, et al., 34–40.

32. Ibid., 24–25; Genot, 276–78; Depoorter, 35; and Message, AMEMBASSY Kinshasa to SECSTATE WASHDC, 05096, DTG 202137Z May 78, Shaba Attack: Military SITREP 2030Z May 20.

33. MMF; Gras, 701–2; Hatte, 29; Message, AMEMBASSY Kinshasa to SECSTATE WASHDC, 05096; and Message, AMEMBASSY Kinshasa to SECSTATE WASHDC, 05090, DTG 201712Z May 78, Shaba Attack: Military SITREP, 1110Z 20 May.

34. MMF; Gras, 702; Sergent, 211–22; Fanshaw, 110; and Erulin, "Objet: Opération Bonité."

35. Depoorter, 35; Genot, 278; and "Sommaire: Kolwezi 78," 30.

36. Ibid.; Legum, *ACR 77–78*, B576–78; and Mangold, 111.

37. Legum, *ACR 77–78*, B578–82; Mangold, 111–12; "Saving a Country From Itself," *Time* (19 June 1978):34; and "U.S. Cobalt Price Jumps," *Aviation Week & Space Technology* (29 May 1978):22.

38. Legum, *ACR 77–78*, B579; Mangold, 113–14; "Zaire Raiders Intent on Mobutu's Ouster," *The New York Times* (24 May 1978); and James Pringle, "Zaire: Signs of Life," *Newsweek* (19 June 1978):49–50. In fact, the FNLC made several more appearances in the region during the remainder of 1978 and into 1979. The loyalty of the province's inhabitants, never very strong, dropped even further with the FAZ's actions after the war was over. The Belgian Paracommando Regiment

repeated its deployment the following year by sending a battalion to Kitona to comfort expatriate fears of further unrest.

39. "French Troops Land in Zaire Battle Zone; U.S. Sees Cuban Role," *The New York Times* (20 May 1978):1, 4; "Belgian-French Rift Over Zaire Reflects Differences in Interests," *The New York Times* (21 May 1978); "Belgians Fear French Intervention in Zaire Is to Expand Influence," *The New York Times* (23 May 1978); and Ronald Koven, "Zaire, Belgium Settle Differences at Surprise Paris Talks," *The Washington Post* (25 May 1978):A4.

40. Mangold, 108–11; and "Carter Criticizes Hill Restraint on U.S. Role Abroad," *The New York Times* (17 May 1978):A1, A25.

41. Crawford Young, "Zaire: The Unending Crisis," *Foreign Affairs* (Fall 1978):181–82; Schmidt, 90; "Saving a Country From Itself," *Time* (29 June 1978):34–35; Mangold, 108–9; Carroll, et al., 39; Legum, *ACR 77–78*, B578; "French Official: Soviet, Cuban Advisors Aiding Zaire Rebels," *The Washington Post* (20 May 1978):A10; Gras, 712–13; "Turmoil in Africa, Will Carter Act?" *U.S. News & World Report* (29 May 1978):17–18; "Castro, Russia's Cat's-Paw," *U.S. News & World Report* (12 June 1978):20–23; "Andrew Young on Africa: Still the Voice of Dissent," *U.S. News & World Report* (12 June 1978):24–25; Joseph Fromm, "Tug of War Over Foreign Policy," *U.S. News & World Report* (19 June 1978):37–40; Raymond Carroll, Paul Martin, and Lars-Erik Nelson, "The Africa Korps," *Newsweek* (19 June 1978):44; "Talking Tough to Moscow," *Time* (19 June 1978):32–33; Angus Deming, Scott Sullivan, Eleanor Clift, and Fred Coleman, "Strong Words for Moscow," *Newsweek* (19 June 1978):41–44; Arnaud de Borchgrave, "Designs on Africa," *Newsweek* (19 June 1978):50. The problem that Carter ran into was one of degree of credibility. The French and, to a lesser extent, the Belgians had supported Mobutu's charges that the Cubans had been involved in the operation. Some had even claimed that the Cubans had been with the FNLC during the operation, a claim never documented. Most observers were willing to accept that the Cubans had provided training to the rebels, who after all had fought with the Cubans and the MPLA during the Angolan Civil War. Where the Carter administration ran into problems was when it seemed to begin equating one form of support with the other without bothering to specify which it was talking about. A skeptical Congress demanded hard evidence before it would support the president in what appeared to be a potential end to détente. The president was not able to satisfy those who questioned the charges. Later, evidence indicated that if any Eastern bloc advisers had been involved, they were probably East Germans.

Chapter 8

1. Erulin, "Objet: Opération Bonité."

2. Malherbe, Letter to General Depoorter.

3. Erulin, "Mission Accomplie," 15.

4. Hatte, 29.

5. Erulin, "Objet: Opération Bonité."

6. "NATO Airlift Deficiencies Seen in Zaire Evacuation," *Aviation Week & Space Technology* (29 May 1978):22; Erulin, "Objet: Opération Bonité"; and "Sommaire: Kolwezi 78," 12–13.

BIBLIOGRAPHY

Books: Primary Sources

Dempster, Chris, and Dave Tomkins. *Fire Power*. New York: St. Martin's Press, 1980.

Erulin, Phillipe, Colonel. *Zaire, Sauver Kolwezi: Un reportage photographique*. Paris: Eric Baschet Éditions, 1979.

Hoare, Mike. *Congo Mercenary*. London: Robert Hale & Co., 1967.

Stockwell, John. *In Search of Enemies: A CIA Story*. New York: W. W. Norton, 1978.

Vandewalle, Frédéric J. L. A. *L'Ommengang: Odyssée et Reconquête de Stanleyville, 1964*. Brussels: Le Livre Africain, Collection Temoinage Africain, 1970.

Books: Secondary Sources

Attwood, William. *The Reds and the Blacks: A Personal Adventure*. New York: Harper & Row, 1967.

Avirgan, Tony, and Martha Honey. *War in Uganda: The Legacy of Idi Amin*. Westport, CT: Lawrence Hill & Co., 1982.

Carlson, Lois. *Monganga Paul*. New York: Harper & Row, 1966.

Conrad, Joseph. *Heart of Darkness* and *The Secret Sharer*. New York: New American Library, 1983.

Davidson, Basil. *The Story of Africa*. London: Mitchell Beasley Publishers and Mitchell Beasley Television, 1984.

Dowdy, Homer E. *Out of the Jaws of the Lion*. New York: Harper & Row, 1965.

Epstein, Howard M., ed. *Revolt in the Congo, 1960–1964*. New York: Facts on File, 1965.

Gran, Guy, with Galen Hull, eds. *Zaire: The Political Economy of Underdevelopment*. New York: Praeger, 1979.

Genot, Émile. *Bérets rouges, Bérets verts . . . 50,000 Paracommandos*. Brussels: Gutenberg Editions, 1986.

Hoyt, Jo Wasson. *For the Love of Mike*. New York: Random House, 1966.

Hymof, Edward. *Stig Von Bayer: International Troubleshooter for Peace*. New York: James H. Heineman, 1965.

Kalb, Madeleine G. *The Congo Cables: The Cold War in Africa—From Eisenhower to Kennedy*. New York: Macmillan Publishing Co., 1982.

Kaplan, Irving, ed. *Zaire: A Country Study*. Washington, DC: American University, 1979.

LeFever, Ernest W., and Wynfred Joshua. *United Nations Peacekeeping in the Congo, 1960–1964: An Analysis of Political, Executive, and Military Control*. 4 vols. Washington, DC: Brookings Institution, 1966.

130

Legum, Colin. "Zaire." In *Africa Contemporary Record: Annual Survey and Documents, 1976–1977*. B534–35. Vol. 9. New York: Africana Publishing Co., 1977.

____. "Zaire." In *Africa Contemporary Record: Annual Survey and Documents, 1977–1978*. B574–90. Vol. 10. New York: Africana Publishing Co., 1979.

____. "Zaire." In *Africa Contemporary Record: Annual Survey and Documents, 1978–1979*. B574–90. Vol. 11. New York: Africana Publishing Co., 1980.

Mezerik, A. G., ed. *Congo and the United Nations*. 3 vols. New York: United Nations International Review Service, 1960–63.

O'Brien, Conor Cruise. *To Katanga and Back: A UN Case History*. New York: Simon & Schuster, 1962.

Odom, Thomas P. *Dragon Operations: Hostage Rescues in the Congo, 1964–1965*. Leavenworth Papers no. 14. Fort Leavenworth, KS: Combat Studies Institute, U.S. Army Command and General Staff College, 1988.

Reed, David. *111 Days in Stanleyville*. New York: Harper & Row, 1965.

Sergent, Pierre. *2éme R.E.P.: Algérie, Tchad, Djibouti, Kolwezi, Beyrouth*. Paris: Presses de la Cité, 1984

____. *Histoire Mondiale des Parachutistes*. Paris: Société de Production Littéraire, 1974.

____. *La Legion*. Barcelona, Spain: SIC SA, 1985.

____. *La Légion Saute sur Kolwezi*. Paris: Presses de la Cité, 1978.

____. *Paras-Légion: Lé 2éme B.E.P. en Indochine*. Paris: Presses de la Cité, 1982.

Thomas, Gerry S. *Mercenary Troops in Modern Africa*. Boulder, CO: Westview Press, 1984.

Vandevoorde, Pierre. *Paras du Monde Entier*. Namur, Belgium: Wesmael-Charlier, 1981.

Wagoner, Fred E. *Dragon Rouge: The Rescue of Hostages in the Congo*. Washington, DC: National Defense University, 1980.

Weissman, Stephen R. *American Foreign Policy in the Congo, 1960–1964*. Ithaca, NY: Cornell University Press, 1965.

Young, John Robert. *The French Foreign Legion: The Inside Story of the World- Famous Fighting Force*. New York: Thames and Hudson, 1984.

Young, Merwin Crawford. *Politics in the Congo: Decolonization and Independence*. Princeton, NJ: Princeton University Press, 1965.

Young, Merwin Crawford, and Thomas Turner. *The Rise and Decline of the Zairian State*. Madison: University of Wisconsin Press, 1985.

Documents: Primary Sources

2éme Régiment Étranger de Parachutistes, État-Major/3éme Bureau. "Ordre Initial D'opérations Concernant L'engagement du 2éme R.E.P. à Kolwezi Par O.A.P. le 19 Mai 78." Kinshasa, 19 May 1978 (0400A).

Erulin, Phillipe, Colonel, Commandant le 2éme Régiment Étranger de Parachutistes, a
Monsieur le Général, Commandant la 11éme Division Parachutiste. "Objet:
Opération Bonité." Calvi, France, 24 June 1978.

Gras, Yves, Colonel, Chef, Mission Militaire Francaise Au Zaire. "Journal de Marche du
13 Mai au 15 Juin 1978."

Lacaze, Général de Division, Commandant la 11éme Division Parachutiste et la 44éme
Division Militaire Territorial a Monsieur le Général Chef d'État-Major de l'Armée
de Terre. "Objet: Opération Bonité" and "Annexe Réflexions sur L'Opération
Bonité." 7 July 1978.

U.S. Department of State. Historical Files: Shaba, Kolwezi, 15–18 May 1978
(approximately 100 messages), Washington, DC.

U.S. European Command. *Lessons Learned From the Logistic Support for the Zaire
Crisis*, 1978, 148–49.

Documents: Secondary Sources

Burkard, Dick J. *Military Airlift Command: Historical Handbook, 1941–1984.* Scott Air
Force Base, IL: Military Airlift Command, U.S. Air Force, 1984.

Malu, Malutama di, Major, Zairian Army. "The Shaba Invasions." Fort Leavenworth,
KS: U.S. Army Command and General Staff College, 1981.

Matthews, James K., and Thomas P. Ofcansky. *Military Airlift Command Operations in
Subsaharan Africa, 1960–1985: A Case Study of Airpower in the Third World.* Scott
Air Force Base, IL: Military Airlift Command, U.S. Air Force, June 1986.

U.S. Congress. House. Subcommittee on Africa of the Committee on International
Relations. *Hearing on United States—Angolan Relations.* 95th Congress, 2d
Session. 25 May 1978.

U.S. Congress. House. Subcommittee on International Security and Scientific Affairs of
the Committee on International Relations. *Hearing on Congressional Oversight of
War Powers Compliance: Zaire Airlift.* 95th Congress, 2d Session. 10 August 1978.

Periodicals: Primary Sources

Chatillon, Christian, Captain. "L'Opération Zaire." *Armées d'Aujourdhui* (July-August
1978):16–17.

Couwenberg, A. "Belgians at Kolwezi—Infantry Letters." *Infantry* (July-August
1980):55.

Depoorter, Henri J. G., Major General, Belgian Army. "Kolwezi." *Military Review*
(September 1979):29–35.

Erulin, Phillipe, Colonel. "Mission Accomplie: Entretien avec le colonel Erulin,
commandant le 2éme R.E.P." *Armées d'Aujourdhui* (July-August 1978):14–15.

Fanshaw, Paul. "Target Kolwezi." *Soldier of Fortune* (December 1983):48–55, 108–12.

Gras, Yves, General. "L'opération Kolwezi." *Mondes et Cultures* 45 (8 November
1985):691–715.

Henrot, Major. "Des vérités bonnes à dire." *Monde* (month unknown, 1978):48–51.

Malherbe, BEM P., Major. "UN Officer Supérieur Belge Temoigne sur Kolwezi: Nous sommes fiers de nos hommes et de notre opération." Newspaper article from unknown Belgian paper, date unknown.

"Sommaire: Kolwezi 78." *Forum de la Force Terrestre.* 8éme Année, No. 3 and 4, September-October 1978.

Periodicals: Secondary Sources

Adelman, Kenneth L. "Old Foes and New Friends." *Africa Report* (January-February 1978):5–10.

"Andrew Young on Africa: Still the Voice of Dissent." *U.S. News & World Report* (12 June 1978):24–25.

"Belgian-French Rift Over Zaire Reflects Differences in Interests." *The New York Times* (21 May 1978):1.

"Belgian Public Opinion Poll Approves Shaba Intervention." *Brussels Special* (14 June 1978) (translated in *JPRS*):8–9.

"Belgians Fear French Intervention in Zaire Is to Expand Influence." *The New York Times* (23 May 1978):1.

Bender, Gerald J. "Angola, the Cubans, and American Anxieties." *Foreign Policy* 31 (Summer 1978):3–30.

Bourchgrave, Arnaud de. "Designs of Africa." *Newsweek* (19 June 1978):50.

Carroll, Raymond, James Pringle, and James O. Goldsborough. "Massacre in Zaire." *Newsweek* (29 May 1978):3–40.

Carroll, Raymond, Paul Martin, and Lars-Erik Nelson. "The Africa Korps." *Newsweek* (19 June 1978):37–40.

"Carter Criticizes Hill Restraints on U.S. Role Abroad." *The New York Times* (17 May 1978):A1, A25.

"Castro: Russia's Cat's-Paw." *U.S. News & World Report* (12 June 1978):20–23.

Champagne, Jacques. "Londres 's'interesse' a l'opération, mais n'y participe pas." *Le Soir* [Brussels] (19 May 1978):3.

The Christian Science Monitor (16, 18, 22 May 1978).

Clerq, Willy de. "Shaba." *Le Soir* [Brussels] (4–5 June 1978) (translated in *JPRS*):1.

"Commentary on Shaba Military Intervention." *La Libre Belgique* (24 May 1978) (translated in *JPRS*):1–4.

Cools, Andre. "Shaba." *Le Soir* [Brussels] (20–21 May 1978) (translated in *JPRS*):1.

Cordy, Jacques. "La France n'entend pas se faire 'pieger' au Zaire, mais se la 'guerre' du Shaba devait s'aggraver. . ." *Le Soir* [Brussels] (18 May 1978):3.

____. "Voler au secours de Mobutu? La France hésite. . ." *Le Soir* [Brussels] (17 May 1978):page unknown.

Crocker, Chester A. "Comment: Making Africa Safe for the Cubans."*Foreign Policy* 31 (Summer 1978):31–33.

D. de M. "Paris: le gouvernement veut garder son sang-froid." *La Libre Belgique* (19 May 1978):3.

Delister, Pierre. "Zaire: On a Medium or Long Term Basis." *Brussels Special* (14 June 1978) (translated in *JPRS*):6–7.

Deming, Angus, Scott Sullivan, Eleanor Clift, and Fred Coleman. "Strong Words for Moscow." *Time* (19 June 1978):41–44.

"Des paras belges et francais sont partis, mais une solution pacifique reste possible." *Le Soir* [Brussels] (19 May 1978):1–3.

"Des soucis ambigus." *La Cité* [Brussels] (18 May 1978):1.

"Embarrassant et Dangereux." *La Libre Belgique* (16 May 1978):1, 4.

Emmanuel, Paul. "Disorganization, Corruption in Kolwezi." *Brussels Special* (21 June 1978) (translated in *JPRS*):58–59.

____."We Will Return to Kolwezi." *Brussels Special* (14 June 1978) (translated in *JPRS*):50–53.

Falony, Robert. "La plus grande prudence." *Le Peuple* [Brussels] (17 May 1978):1.

Fooz, Alain de. "Are We Prepared?" *Brussels Special* (12 June 1978) (translated in *JPRS*):10–12.

"French Official: Soviet, Cuban Advisors Aiding Zaire Rebels." *The Washington Post* (20 May 1978):A10.

"French Troops Land in Zaire Battle Zone; U.S. Sees Cuban Role." *The New York Times* (20 May 1978):1, 4.

Fromm, Joseph. "Tug of War Over Foreign Policy." *U.S. News & World Report* (19 June 1978):37–40.

Haquin, Rene. "Melbroeck: une larme au fusil." *Le Soir* [Brussels] (19 May 1978):3.

Hatte, Jaques, Lieutenant Colonel, French Army. "Kolwezi: An Airborne Assault." *Infantry* (May 1979):25–29.

"How African War Is Hitting Home in Cuba." *U.S. News & World Report* (19 June 1978):45–47.

"Inquiétude sur le sort des Européens a Kolwezi." *La Libre Belgique* (17 May 1978):1, 4.

"Irritation zairoise contre M. Simonet." *La Libre Belgique* (19 May 1978).

"Jump Into Shaba!" Translated from *Kept Blanc, Soldier of Fortune* (February 1979):56–58.

J. v. C. "L'intervention belge à Stanleyville en novembre 1964." *Le Soir* [Brussels] (17 May 1978).

Kazadi, F. S. B. "Mobutu, MPR, and the Politics of Survival." *Africa Report* (January-February 1978):11–16.

Kiesel, Frédéric. "Des soucis ambigus." *La Cité* [Brussels] (18 May 1978):1.

Koven, Ronald. "Zaire, Belgium Settle Differences at Surprise Paris Talks." *The Washington Post* (25 May 1978):A4.

"La bataille pour Kolwezi: un enjeu vital pour le gouvernement zairois." *Le Soir* [Brussels] (14–16 May 1978):3 (in each edition).

"L'aeroport de Kolwezi: declassé...." *Le Soir* [Brussels] (19 May 1978):3.

"La situation au Shaba prime toutes les autres préoccupations gouvernementales." *Le Peuple* [Brussels] (19 May 1978):1.

"Le drame de Kolwezi met le gouvernement a l'épreuve." *Le Soir* [Brussels] (20 May 1978):2.

"Le Fil des Événements, Rue de la Loi." *La Libre Belgique* (19 May 1978).

Legum, Colin. "It's Germans, Not Cubans." *The New Republic* (June 1978):8.

____. "The African Crisis." *Foreign Affairs: America and the World* (1978): 633–51.

"Les C-130: des appareils a tous usages." *Le Soir* [Brussels] (19 May 1978):3.

"Les Européens de Kolwezi pris dans les combats et poursuivis par la haine des ex-gendarmes." *La Libre Belgique* (19 May 1978).

"L'opération de sauvetage des Européens de Kolwezi sera-t-elle nécessaire?" *La Libre Belgique* (19 May 1978):1.

Malumo, Siyanga. "Another Close Shave for Mobutu." *Africa* (No. 83, July 1978):50–52.

Mangold, Peter. "Shaba I and Shaba II." *Survival* 21 (May-June 1979):107–15.

Marks, Thomas A. "The Shaba Adventure." *Africa Institute Bulletin* 16 (No. 3, 1978):111–15.

"Massacre in Zaire." *U.S. News & World Report* (5 June 1978):41–42.

"M. Henri Simonet à la Chambre: il ne s'agirait pas d'une immixation." *Le Soir* [Brussels] (18 May 1978):3.

"Mobutu demande l'aide étrangère pour faire face a l'invasion du Shaba." *Le Soir* [Brussels] (14–16 May 1978):1, 3 (in all editions).

"Most Americans Said to Leave War Zone." *The New York Times* (18 May 1978):A3.

"M. Simonet: pas d'intervention militaire belge." *Le Soir* [Brussels] (14–16 May 1978):3 (in all editions).

"NATO Airlift Deficiencies Seen in Zaire Evacuation." *Aviation Week & Space Technology* (29 May 1978):22.

The New York Times (15–24, 26 May; 1, 3, 5–7, 10, 16 June; 11 July 1978).

Nudelhole, Susa. "Gendarmes." *Le drapeau rouge* [Brussels] (17 May 1978):1.

Ogunbadejo, Oye. "Conflict in Africa: A Case Study of the Shaba Crisis, 1977." *World Affairs* 141 (Winter 1979):219–34.

"Paras belges et francais au Zaire; Pour la France le sauvetage concernerait aussi les Zairois." *Le Soir* [Brussels] (19 May 1978):3.

"Paras belges et francais ont commencé une opération de sauvetage." *La Dernière Heure* (19 May 1978):28.

"Paris: le gouvernement veut garder son sang-froid." *La Libre Belgique* (19 May 1978):3.

"Political Party Positions (Summary)." *La Libre Belgique* (24 May 1978) (translated in *JPRS*):4.

"Préoccupation no. 1: l'évacuation éventuelle des Occidentaux de Kolwezi." *Le Soir* [Brussels] (18 May 1978):3.

Pringle, James. "Zaire: Signs of Life." *Newsweek* (19 June 1978):49–50.

Sana, Kyenga. "Kolwezi Liberated." *Brussels Special* (29 May 1978) (translated in *JPRS*):10–12.

Sauldie, Madan. "France's Military Intervention in Africa." *Africa* (No. 77, January 1978):43–49.

"Saving a Country From Itself." *Time* (19 June 1978):34–35.

Schmidt, Rudolf. "Zaire After the 1978 Shaba Crisis." *Aussen Politik*, English edition 30 (1st Quarter 1979):88–99.

"Shaba C'est L'aventure Néo-Coloniale." *Le drapeau rouge* [Brussels] (19 May 1978):1.

"S'il faut sauver les Européens bloqués à Kolwezi, les mesures nécessaires ont été prises." *Le Soir* [Brussels] (18 May 1978):1, 3.

"Strong Words for Moscow." *Newsweek* (19 June 1978).

"Talking Tough to Moscow." *Time* (29 June 1978):32–33.

"Toute l'Afrique concernée par le Shaba." *Le Soir* [Brussels] (17 May 1978):3.

"Turmoil in Africa: Will Carter Act?" *U.S. News & World Report* (29 May 1978):7–19.

"Une extrême préoccupation." *Le Soir* [Brussels] (18 May 1978):3.

Unwin, Francis. "Des paras belges et francais sont partis, mais une solution pacifique reste possible." *Le Soir* [Brussels] (19 May 1978):1–3.

"U.S. Cobalt Price Jumps." *Aviation Week & Space Technology* (29 May 1978):22.

"U.S. Set to Evacuate 73 Citizens in Zaire." *The New York Times* (17 May 1978):A2, A8.

Vankeerbergen, Jean-Paul. "La canonnière." *Le drapeau rouge* [Brussels] (18 May 1978):4.

Van Nieuwenhuyse, Henri. "Decision au Shaba, Devant l'inevitable." *La Dernieère Heure* [Brussels] (19 May 1978):1.

____. "Les tenailles sovietiques." *La Dernière Heure* [Brussels] (17 May 1978):1.

The Washington Post (15–22, 24–26, 29 May 1978).

Young, Crawford. "Zaire: The Unending Crisis." *Foreign Affairs* (Fall 1978):169–85.

"Zaire: Foreign Legion Intervenes in Shaba." *Africa* (June 1978):27–29.

"Zaire Raiders Intent on Mobutu's Ouster." *The New York Times* (24 May 1978):A1.

Other Sources

Erulin, Phillipe, Colonel. "Kolwezi." Script to a presentation at the U.S. Army War College, Carlisle Barracks, PA, date unknown.

Malherbe, BEM P., Colonel. Commander, Paracommando Regiment, Belgian Army. Interview with the author, Everberg, Belgium, 24 November 1988.

___. Letter to General Depoorter Concerning Kolwezi, March 1981.

☆ U.S. GOVERNMENT PRINTING OFFICE: 1993 — 7 5 5 _ 0 0 1 / 8 2 0 0 2

www.ingramcontent.com/pod-product-compliance
Lightning Source LLC
Chambersburg PA
CBHW060435090426
42733CB00011B/2287